$\dfrac{40}{\text{Misc.}}$
990

MEMORANDUM ON THE TREATMENT OF

INJURIES IN WAR

BASED ON EXPERIENCE OF THE PRESENT CAMPAIGN.

JULY, 1915.

LONDON:
PRINTED UNDER THE AUTHORITY OF HIS MAJESTY'S STATIONERY OFFICE
BY HARRISON AND SONS, 45–47, ST. MARTIN'S LANE, W.C.,
PRINTERS IN ORDINARY TO HIS MAJESTY.

1915.

FireStep Editions

FireStep Publishing
Gemini House
136-140 Old Shoreham Road
Brighton
BN3 7BD

www.firesteppublishing.com

First published by the General Staff, War Office 1915.
First published in this format by FireStep Editions,
an imprint of FireStep Publishing, in association with
the National Army Museum, 2013.

NATIONAL
ARMY
MUSEUM

www.nam.ac.uk

ISBN 978-1-908487-91-9

Cover design FireStep Publishing
Typeset by FireStep Publishing
Printed and bound in Great Britain

Please note: *In producing in facsimile from original historical documents, any
imperfections may be reproduced and the quality may be lower than modern
typesetting or cartographic standards.*

SCOPE OF MEMORANDUM.

These memoranda have been drawn up with a view to summarising the experience gained in the Military Hospitals in France during the past ten months, and to attaining some uniformity in methods of treatment based upon definite observation.

The recommendations are designed to meet the conditions under which the Medical Service has been working, as to (a) the actual character of the wounds, and some special features dependent on climatic conditions, environment, and new methods of warfare ; (b) the primary transport of sick and wounded men from the field ; and (c) the rapid transference of patients to England, which restricts the treatment of any individual case to a limited period of its course.

Any attempt to cover the whole field of military medicine and surgery would obviously be impracticable even if desirable, and the memoranda are, therefore, for the most part confined to remarks on indications and methods of practical procedure in certain classes of case. Where necessary it has been attempted to draw a distinction between methods suitable for the Front and the Base respectively.

The conditions of this campaign have resulted in the surgical treatment of patients being divided up into more or less distinct stages :—

(1) That at the field ambulances and casualty clearing stations.

(2) That at the various medical bases in France.

(3) At the actual medical base in England. For this reason it has been impossible to use the term "General Hospital" in this memorandum.

A. T. SLOGGETT,
D.G.

TABLE OF CONTENTS.

(B 11379) Wt. w. 7097—2500 12M 7/15 H & S P15/403

PAGES

LIST OF ILLUSTRATIONS.

WOUNDS AT FIELD AMBULANCES AND CASUALTY CLEARING STATIONS.

THE CONDITION OF WOUNDED MEN.

The majority of gunshot wounds do not inflict very serious injury, and so do not cause material shock or collapse, but in every convoy of wounded there are always some men in a serious state of collapse. This may result from one or more of several causes :—(1) Excessive bleeding. (2) Long exposure to cold, wet, and hunger, as when men cannot be rescued because of heavy fire. (3) Serious visceral injury to the chest or abdomen. (4) Extensive shell wounds, especially when associated with fracture of the long bones, and particularly of the femur. (5) The infliction of multiple injuries by shells or bombs. Whatever may be the cause or causes of collapse, the patient is always made worse by the journey in an ambulance wagon, especially if the limbs are fractured. In these circumstances it is generally best to allow him to rest quietly for an hour or two before attempting to dress his wounds, or even to examine him. Many men who are collapsed are sick and cannot take solid food, but small quantities of water or brandy should be frequently given if possible, and if hot milk and soup can be taken they are to be preferred to alcohol. Plenty of water is good if the patient is not sick. If food is not tolerated, ten to twenty ounces of warm saline, with the addition of 10 per cent glucose, should be given per rectum, while if collapse is very severe, especially if it is due to hæmorrhage, normal

[marginal notes:] General. Effects of gunshot injuries.

General treatment.

saline solution should be given subcutaneously, intravenously, or continuously per rectum. Pituitary extract has been found very useful in many cases.

An injection of antitetanic serum is to be given to every wounded man. (*See* Tetanus, p. 16.)

THE DRESSING OF WOUNDS.

First field dressing.

It is of the utmost importance that the *first field dressing should always be removed as soon as possible*. It has in many cases been applied by the soldier himself or by his comrades, it has been soiled by contact with dirty clothes and dirty hands, and it is often applied to a dirty skin. It has almost always been put on too tightly if applied by unskilled persons, and even if not put on too tightly, the swelling of an injured limb may soon make the bandage too tight. It has also been found that very frequent changes of dressings are most necessary, and that gangrene is specially liable to occur if a wound is left in contact with muddy clothing or with dressings soaked in blood or other discharge.

Procedure at the Field Ambulance.

If the patient is on a stretcher soiled with blood or mud he should be removed from it before exposing the wound, and placed on a clean stretcher, for a foul stretcher will quickly contaminate the dressings and wound.

Both medical officers and orderlies should wear clean aprons or gowns, and sterile rubber gloves should be worn if wounds are explored with the finger, or opened up for drainage, or other manipulation.

CLEANSING THE WOUND AND ITS SURROUNDINGS.

The first step is to remove all clothing from the injured part, to place the limb upon sterile jaconet, waterproof sheeting or a towel, and cover the wound with an antiseptic swab, in order to protect it from further contact with dirt. If there be a clean small wound caused by a rifle or shrapnel bullet it is only necessary to wash off dirt and blood from the wound, and from a large area of surrounding skin.

If it be an open wound, portions of clothing, obvious fragments of shell, and torn or hopelessly damaged portions of tissue should be removed by forceps and scissors. If the wound be not sufficiently open to drain of itself, large drainage tubes should be inserted; and in cases where more must be done an anæsthetic should be given, and the wounds enlarged and held open by retractors so that all recesses may be washed out and drained. A good method of mechanically cleaning the track of a perforating wound consists in drawing backwards and forwards through it a piece of gauze twisted to form a rope. Very large drainage tubes ($\frac{5}{8} - \frac{7}{8}$ inch) should be used, with numerous large lateral openings. For large deep wounds counter-openings are necessary. *(Method of cleansing the wound.)*

Hæmorrhage.—Neither bullet nor shell wounds usually bleed much in those patients who reach a field ambulance or a clearing station, for if hæmorrhage has continued from a large vessel, the bleeding is in most cases rapidly fatal. If, however, there is obvious hæmorrhage from an artery in an open wound this should be tied; but if there is only bleeding from the track of a bullet, this can nearly always be arrested by careful firm bandaging over a splint. If this is insufficient, the wound may be plugged in addition, but plugging is liable to encourage septic infection and gaseous cellulitis, and should only be resorted to in case of urgent necessity. *(Treatment of hæmorrhage. Plugging of wounds.)*

Hæmorrhage should be arrested if possible in the field ambulance.

If bleeding has been arrested by plugging the wound, a special note of this should be sent with the patient for the information of the medical officer to whose care he is consigned.

If the bleeding is evidently arterial, and copious, the wound should be enlarged under an anæsthetic, and the bleeding vessel sought for and tied. It is hardly ever permissible to tie a main artery in continuity on the proximal side of the bleeding point at a distance from the wound. If a tourniquet has been applied on the field, this should always be removed *as soon as possible* in every case, otherwise gangrene is easily caused. If no bleeding follows removal of the tourniquet nothing more should be done. If bleeding recurs the treatment advised above should be adopted. It is quite wrong to leave a tourniquet applied for several hours, and a note should always accompany a case in which a tourniquet is in place, lest it be overlooked.

Use of tourniquets.

Application of Antiseptics. — Experience has been disappointing as to the efficacy of any antiseptic medium to inhibit bacterial growth within the fouled wounds produced either by shell fragments, or shrapnel, or by rifle bullets where the apertures of entry and exit depart from the simplest type. It has, moreover, shown that any medium is to be avoided which produces extensive coagula, and tends to block free exit of the wound discharges.

Observation of a very large number of cases has on the other hand shown that the provision of *adequate drainage* suffices to prevent any serious general or local extension of infection which has already occurred, and in conjunction with the mechanical methods of cleansing *forms the essential element in the primary treatment of gunshot wounds.*

Importance of drainage.

The following antiseptic preparations have been found useful in the primary treatment of the wound. Prior to the application of any of them, the surface of the wound should be dried by a swab and rendered entirely free of blood :—

A 2 per cent solution of iodine in spirit. This solution is useful for application to superficial wounds, and to the surrounding skin. For the interior of deep dirty wounds it is not advisable. It should not be applied to the skin in cases of injury to the spinal cord or peripheral nerves. In such cases it is apt to give rise to vesication and subsequent sores. *Antiseptics recommended.*

Solutions of carbolic acid in the strength of $2\frac{1}{2}$ per cent to 5 per cent. Lysol solution (1 drachm to 1 pint). Solution of biniodide or perchloride of mercury (1-1000) are also used.

Hydrogen peroxide solution (5–10 volumes) has been extensively employed in wounds fouled with soil, and is often used as a preliminary to the application of one of the other forms of antiseptics or mixed with them.

A 1 per cent watery solution of picric acid is a useful and anodyne application for the multiple superficial wounds caused by small fragments of high explosive shells or bombs and by the dirt and stones which they drive in.

Dressing of the Wound.—Small and superficial wounds should be dressed with dry, antiseptic gauze ; such wounds, especially when treated with 2 per cent iodine solution, usually arrive at the base hospitals clean, and covered by a firm dark scab.

For extensive and foul wounds a moist dressing is to be preferred. The following are suitable solutions for moistening the gauze : 1-60 carbolic lotion to which has been added 5 per cent of sodium chloride ;

Lysol 1 drachm to 1 pint ; or 1–2000 mercuric chloride or biniodide. In wounds of this nature every effort must be made to afford free egress to the discharges. The **Drainage of the wounds.** large drainage tube with lateral openings if it does not pass across the limb must be fixed in position, if necessary by a suture, the whole length of the wound should be kept open, the dressing should be applied lightly, and in no case should impermeable tissue such as jaconet be placed on the surface. Winding gauze from a roll around a limb with multiple injuries is objectionable, as the blood dries and tightens the bandage. Where a splint is applied, the dressings and bandage should, if possible, be so arranged as to allow of renewal without removal of the splint, *and no bandage of any kind should be applied to a fractured limb except over a splint.* Many-tailed bandages are very useful for this purpose.

Sutures must not be introduced, since experience has shown that all wounds must be regarded as infected.

Immobilization of limbs. The importance of immobilization of the limb in checking the spread of infection and diffusion into the general circulation in cases other than fractures of the bones must be borne in mind. All wounds of joints, and limbs with extensive lacerated wounds should be fixed by the application of splints.

ON THE FILLING UP OF TALLIES.

Much trouble has been caused on the arrival of cases in casualty clearing stations, stationary and general hospitals by the incompleteness of the details inscribed on the tallies.

Observance of the following rules will much facilitate the work of the hospitals to which the patient is transferred :—

All tallies should bear—

1. The stamp of the Unit through which the case has been passed.
2. An *accurate* description of the injury, for example— "Compound fracture of skull," not " G.S.W. head." "Compound fracture of femur," not " Shrapnel wound of leg."
3. Time of last dressing.
4. Concise account of any operation performed.
5. Amount of tetanus antitoxin injected.
6. Whether morphia has been administered and in what amount.

SUBSEQUENT TREATMENT OF WOUNDS.

In the later stages no essential deviation from the rules above enunciated is to be made, but the arrival of a patient at a base hospital allows of a wider variation of the methods by which they may be applied.

In the large wounds a second process of mechanical cleansing is usually required. To the employment of the gauze swab and scissors, the use of a blunt spoon may now be added, as it removes the disintegrating blood-clot, muscle and soft tissues well. Free removal of dead tissue is very important. *(Secondary cleansing of wounds.)*

Where tension exists further incisions may be necessary, especially in the case of anaerobic infections, although if the incisions and primary drainage have been free enough they should not often be required. In the subcutaneous tissue these measures suffice to arrest the progress of the infection. When the deep tissues are involved the introduction of additional large drainage tubes is required. Gauze wicks should never be used for this purpose. Several openings of moderate size along *(Secondary incisions.)*

the course of extension of the infection are as a rule to be preferred to one large incision, both as avoiding the production of a wide fresh surface to the infective wound discharges and also as curtailing the period required for cicatrisation. Again, the process of dressing is rendered less painful.

Avoidance of pain during changes of dressing.

The pain accompanying the dressing of large open wounds has been a cause of constant solicitude. Where a large cutaneous margin is exposed, the application of a strip of gauze or lint spread with soft boracic ointment or vaseline has been found useful in facilitating the removal of dressings, especially in amputation stumps. The direct application of a thin sheet of rubber tissue to the whole wound surface has also been tried with success.

Excision of wounds and secondary suture.

As a step in the secondary cleansing of wounds it is often desirable to remove the contused and sloughing margin of skin. At this stage, or usually a little later, certain wounds may with advantage be excised, and the edges brought together by deep sutures ; by this means time is saved and a better cosmetic result attained, but great care must be taken in the selection of the case and to ensure asepsis.

Use of antiseptic media.

At this period of treatment the application of powerful antiseptic media to the wound is undesirable. Any of the solutions already referred to may be employed, but it should be remarked that a large concensus of opinion on the part of competent observers favours the principle laid down and advocated by Sir Almroth Wright, that the course of healing is most effectively furthered by means tending to increase the activity of the vital processes concerned in its production. The main feature in the method of wound treatment propounded by Wright is the promotion of a free outflow of lymph, favourable to phagocytic activity and inimical to microbes, from the tissues into the wound. This outflow, "lymph lavage," is encouraged by the application of hypertonic solutions of sodium chloride.

"For ordinary use the best application will be a 5 per cent solution of common salt combined with ½ per cent citrate of soda to render the lymph incoagulable. Where citrate of soda, or a similar decalcifiant, is not available a simple 5 per cent solution of salt will serve.—In dealing with dry and infiltrated wound surfaces stronger solutions of salt (up to 10 per cent) will be found to resolve the induration and to clean up the wound surfaces much more quickly than weaker solutions." *(margin note: Hypertonic solutions of common salt.)*

"The hypertonic solution or 'drawing agent' has done its work as soon as it has checked the spreading invasion of the tissues ; or has cleaned up the dry and indurated wound surface, and this last has clothed itself in bright coral red granulations. The hypertonic salt solution may then be replaced by some simple dressing."*

For work in military hospitals, the pure substitution of hypertonic solution of sodium chloride for all antiseptic media cannot be considered safe or advisable, hence it is recommended that a "Hypertonic Solution" (5 per cent sodium chloride and ½ per cent sodium citrate) should form the basis to which the addition of carbolic acid (2 per cent) forms a convenient complement. *(margin note: Combination of a hypertonic solution and an antiseptic recommended.)*

Soloids of sodium chloride and citrate may be placed in the wound, and this measure has found some favour.

Hypertonic solutions such as (1) a saturated solution of glucose containing 1 in 80 carbolic acid (Whitehouse), or (2) 1 in 60 carbolic acid with 30 per cent. of glycerine have also been employed with success.

---

* Memorandum on the treatment of bacterial infections of projectile wounds, issued to all medical units in April, 1915.

Gauze moistened by one of these solutions should be lightly introduced into the open wound, and a few layers applied to the surface. The flow of lymph induced by the presence of the hypertonic solution is probably thus furthered by both capillary attraction and the absorbent qualities of the gauze itself. The dressing should either lie loosely, or be very lightly fixed in position.

Hydrogen peroxide.

In the early stages hydrogen peroxide solution offers some advantages for irrigation of the wounds, beyond its possible bactericidal powers, by reason of its mechanical action in separating débris from the wound surface. For superficial wounds the best method of application is by means of a spraying bottle, and used in this manner the solution is most valuable in facilitating the removal of adherent wound dressings, and avoiding pain to the patient. It has been found that the addition of $2\frac{1}{2}$ per cent carbolic acid greatly increases its disinfecting properties (Parry Morgan). Prolonged use of hydrogen peroxide solution is undesirable, as it tends to produce a pale flabby type of granulation.

Iodoform.

Iodoform has proved an efficacious application to sloughy wounds, especially those in which anaerobic infection is or has been present.

Necessity for change of applications during course of healing.

It should be remembered, whatever form of application is adopted, that a change from time to time is beneficial or necessary when the granulating process fails in activity. This remark applies to the "hypertonic" treatment equally with every other.

In foul wounds and in all where discharge is abundant, the importance of frequent dressing of the wound is obvious.

Continuous baths.

Baths.—For deep, sloughy wounds of the limbs, baths have proved efficacious. Iodine water (tinct. iodi. 1 drachm to 1 pint); hypertonic saline solution (5 per cent sodium

chloride with ½ per cent sodium citrate) with the
addition of 2 per cent carbolic acid ; or lysol (1 drachm to
1 pint), are good forms. Immersion for a period of one
to two hours once or twice a day is sufficient, after which
a moist dressing should be used.

Continuous Irrigation.—The above solutions may be
employed for continuous irrigation in positions in which
a bath is impracticable, and especially when the object is
to remove accumulating pus. In the latter case the
hypertonic solution is especially applicable. Continuous
irrigation is most likely to prove of service in the treatment of superficial wounds or deep wounds with a large
external opening, and is then best applied by arranging a
slow drip on to a thin layer of gauze. It is practically
useless to pass a current of fluid through drainage tubes
which cross a limb, or which have lain in a track for
many hours, even though lateral openings are present in
the tube. It should be borne in mind that the evapora-
tion from the wound surface accompanying the process of
irrigation has a tendency to produce depression and
exhaustion of the patient, hence the method must be used
with care and due consideration of the strength of the
patient concerned. Continuous irrigation.

Exposure to the air and sun.—When wounds have
reached the stage of pronounced granulation, exposure to
the air and sun under suitable climatic conditions may
hasten healing. If this method be employed a thin veil
of gauze should be used, moistened with an antiseptic
solution to which glycerine (1 oz. to 1 pint) has been
added to prevent undesirable desiccation of the wound,
and it need hardly be added that means must be taken to
avoid the access of flies. It is in the treatment of wounds
that have acquired an atonic character that this method
is most useful. Exposure to air and sun.

Removal of Foreign Bodies.—The immediate removal of rifle bullets from any but the most accessible positions is always to be deprecated, and even when these lie close beneath the skin they are better left until the arrival of a patient at a base hospital, since the production of a fresh wound prior to a period of transport is most undesirable. The above rule applies in a slightly lesser degree to shrapnel balls, although here the probability of the simultaneous introduction of portions of clothing is greater. Fragments of shrapnel shell cases, and of bombs or high explosive shells fall into a different category, since they carry with them not only fragments of clothing, but also considerable amounts of soil. Where feasible without an extensive operation, their removal should form a portion of the process of primary cleansing of the wound. They should, in any case, be extracted at the base hospital as soon as they have been located by X-ray examination, unless their removal involves grave immediate risks, as in the case of the great body cavities.

(margin: Removal of foreign bodies.)

GAS-GANGRENE AND GASEOUS CELLULITIS.

(margin: Organisms concerned.)

The most important complication of wounds in this war is their infection by anaerobic organisms derived from dung. The chief are the bacillus of malignant œdema and the Bacillus perfringens, or Bacillus aerogenes capsulatus. The majority of all open wounds contain one or more of these organisms, but it is only exceptionally that they give rise to massive gangrene. The conditions which favour the development of gangrene may be thus summarised:—(a) The retention of extravasated blood and of wound secretions, (b) interference with the circulation, (c) the presence of large masses of partially devitalized or dead tissue, (d) extensive

(margin: Conditions favouring occurrence of gangrene.)

fracture and comminution of the long bones, (e) the soaking with blood of dressings or clothes which are left in contact with the wound for a long time.

It is evident, therefore, that tightly applied bandages, infrequently changed dressings, and imperfectly drained wounds all predispose to gangrene. In many cases of extensive shell or bullet wounds it occurs as the result of the extensive crushing of the tissues, and, if a limb dies from injury to its main vessels, gas-gangrene inevitably supervenes very quickly.

The gangrene may commence as a local infection with spread of gas in the tissues, and especially the sub-cutaneous tissue around the wound, or the whole limb may be rapidly infected and may die "en masse" in a few hours. In either case the patient may be poisoned by absorption from the infected tissues, or a hæmic infection may develop. Gas-gangrene usually occurs within the first two or three days after the infliction of a wound, but it may begin within a few hours, or be delayed for several days. It may also become manifest after a latent period during which the wound has appeared to be doing well. Its onset is often extremely rapid, and a limb whose condition has given rise to no anxiety in the evening may be found in a state of advanced gangrene next morning. *Course of the disease.*

Modes of onset.

In the milder cases the tissues around the wound are found to crackle to the touch as they do when surgical emphysema complicates a wounded lung. This is due to the development of gas, which, in the absence of treatment, spreads rapidly over the whole affected limb, and may invade the trunk within 24 hours or less. On account of the gas in the tissues such a limb is tympanitic on percussion. In such cases the circulation in the hand or foot is not at first affected.

In a second class the whole limb becomes greatly
swollen and very tense, and at first extremely painful.
It quickly becomes livid or purple, and later the colour
changes to a dark green or black. The hand or foot is
cold and numbed to all sense of touch, the pulse is absent
and the part quickly dies.

In either type the wound secretes a dark, dirty fluid,
bubbling with gas, which has a characteristic and extremely foul odour, and true pus is never present. In
later stages the fluid is brilliant orange, and makes a
stain of this colour on the dressings.

In milder types, mainly those of gaseous cellulitis, the
condition of the patient may be quite good for some time
after the infective process has begun.

In the second class, although the patient may be quite
alert mentally and does not complain of feeling very ill,
his pulse is of very low tension, often very small and
rapid, or even imperceptible, his hands and feet are cold,
his tongue is dried and furred, and vomiting and hiccough
are frequent complications. The temperature is often
sub-normal and is never materially raised. A sudden fall
to a sub-normal temperature is a very bad prognostic
sign. Death usually occurs within the first 48 hours,
but some patients survive for several days.

Treatment.—The general indications consist in the
removal of as much blood clot and devitalized tissue as
possible, provision of free access to the air, and efficient
drainage.

Any wound that shows local signs of gaseous cellulitis
should be freely opened under an anæsthetic, dead skin
or muscle should be cut away, and the whole wound
should be most thoroughly cleansed by mopping it out
with gauze and an antiseptic till every part of it is completely cleaned. Hydrogen peroxide is specially advised

by many surgeons, and may be used in conjunction with other antiseptics. Suitable drainage tubes should be inserted, and the wound either dressed with some form of moist compress or left exposed to the constant application of hypertonic salt solution. If the neighbouring cellular tissue is gaseous and crackling it must be incised and treated like the wound. If the hand or foot is warm and sensitive, amputation should not as a rule be performed.

In the second and worst class, where the swollen and discoloured limb dies, and the hand or foot is cold and numb, amputation should be performed at once if the condition of the patient permits it. In many such cases, however, and especially when the thigh is affected by a compound fracture, the patient is often too ill, and amputation is evidently useless and should not be done. The cases which do the best are those where the gangrene is primarily due to injury to the main vessel of the limb, and many of those recover if amputation is not delayed. Recovery occurs in some cases even when the operation is done through infected tissue, but the flaps should always be cut very short, or a simple transverse section of the limb should be made.

Amputa-tion.

TETANUS.

The heavily-manured soil of the districts in which fighting has occurred frequently contains the spores of tetanus bacilli ; these, in many wounds, are driven deep into the tissues and may find there the anaerobic conditions suitable for their development. Should the bacilli establish themselves in such a wound they give rise to toxins which have a great affinity for nervous tissue and produce the well-known symptoms of the disease.

PREVENTION.

Primary treatment of the wound.

(A.) **General measures.**—The steps advocated in other parts of this pamphlet for the cleaning, dressing and drainage of freshly received wounds, as well as for their appropriate surgical treatment, with a view to minimising the risks of sepsis, are those which, if fully carried out, will also minimise the risk of tetanus. They need not, therefore, be further described here.

(B.) **Special measures.**—These resolve themselves into the prophylactic use of tetanus antitoxin, a proceeding of well-established value.

Prophylactic use of Tetanus Antitoxin.—Since in the first two months of the war more cases of tetanus occurred than had been anticipated, either by ourselves or our Allies, it was decided to direct that a preventive dose of serum should be given to every wounded man, in place of leaving this, as had been done at first, to the discretion of the medical officer. The results have been excellent and, in the last six months, there have only been 36 cases of the disease among those who received a preventive dose of serum within 24 hours of being wounded. That this is not due to the possible absence of the cause of infection from the soil is clear from the following facts. (1) Bacteriological examination of the wounds has often proved the presence of tetanus bacilli, although no tetanic symptoms have followed. (2) Many instances of slight trismus, or of localised tetanic spasms of a muscle or a group of muscles, have been reported, without the subsequent development of generalised tetanus. (3) 34 cases of severe tetanus have been reported in this period among the very small fraction of wounded men who, for one reason or another, had not received a preventive dose of the serum within 24 hours. (4) A considerable number of wounded horses continue to develop the disease.

The general use of preventive inoculation of the serum has also had an effect on the severity of the symptoms, if, in spite of the preventive dose, the disease should subsequently develop. For example, of the 34 cases mentioned above, which did not have a preventive dose within 24 hours, 32 died, a case-mortality of 94·1 per cent. ; whereas, of the 36 cases which occurred among the enormously larger class of wounded who *had* received a preventive dose, 28 died, a case-mortality of 77·7 per cent. *Results of preventive inoculation.*

The preventive dose of 500 units should be given subcutaneously at a distance from the wound at the earliest possible moment, and the fact of inoculation, as well as the size of the dose, should invariably be recorded on the "tally." In severe wounds medical officers not infrequently give 1,500 units ; there is no objection to this, but, at the same time, there is no evidence that the smaller dose is insufficient, if given promptly. *Importance of record on "tally."*

It should be remembered that injuries other than those caused by bullets or shells may also become infected ; several fatal cases have followed trivial injuries, for which *Gunshot wounds not sole gate of infection.*

the soldier did not report sick at the time, and others have followed on the gangrene due to frost-bite. It would be wise to give a preventive dose in all instances in which the danger of infection of a wound with contaminated soil may be presumed to exist.

Several different preparations of tetanus antitoxin are in use. These have all been recently tested, and in each case they were found to contain at least the number of units claimed.

(The question of Anaphylaxis is dealt with below.)

Influence of the duration of the Incubation period on the severity of the attack.—The general experience has been, as was to be expected, that the shorter the interval between the receipt of the wound and the appearance of the symptoms, the smaller the chance of recovery. At the same time, cases have recovered in which the symptoms appeared 6 days after the wound, and cases have proved fatal where 19 days had elapsed. The average incubation period of 43 fatal cases was 8·83 days, and that of 26 cases which recovered was 11·57 days.

Average incubation period.

TREATMENT WHEN THE DISEASE IS ESTABLISHED.

Mortality.

A careful study has been made of 179 cases in which certain particulars which had been called for were furnished. Of these 179 cases 140 have died, a case-mortality of 78·2 per cent. Although this figure is disappointingly high, it must not be forgotten that the majority of these cases were also suffering from severe forms of sepsis, and, in a considerable number of them, the reporting officer stated that the tetanic symptoms had completely subsided under treatment, the patient dying from septicæmia, gangrene, secondary hæmorrhage or other causes.

(A.) **Local and surgical measures.**—Steps should be taken to open up and clean the wound, if this has not already been done, and the freest possible drainage should be secured. The local application of strong antiseptics, swabbing with pure carbolic acid, the free use of hydrogen peroxide, and similar measures, have been tried, but appear to have had little influence on the course of the disease. Surgical interference of a grave nature, such as amputation of a limb, has been carried out in a number of instances, but such cases have almost always died, though not necessarily from the severity of the tetanic symptoms.

(B.) **General measures.**—The patient should be kept in a perfectly quiet and darkened room, maintained, as far as possible, at an equable temperature. The avoidance of all external stimuli, likely to start a spasm, is to be aimed at, and some have advocated the bandaging of the eyes, the plugging of the ears with wool, the placing of the feet of the bed on rubber discs, etc., with this object in view. It is of great importance to maintain the strength of the patient by means of adequate fluid nourishment, given in small quantities at frequent intervals, and by the rectum if swallowing tends to induce spasm.

(C.) **The use of anæsthetics and sedatives.**—As regards the former, chloroform is most commonly used, though ether has been preferred by some, especially when required for a small operation or for the dressing of a painful wound. Their value is well recognized. As sedatives, chloral hydrate, potassium bromide and morphia are most frequently used for the purpose of controlling spasm, the first-named being the most valuable. They are of undoubted value in this direction but do not appear to modify the course of the disease to any great extent. Too frequent or too large doses may do harm. Chloretone, in doses of 30-40 grains in olive oil, given by the rectum, has been well spoken of for the same purpose of controlling spasm.

(D.) **Carbolic acid method.**—This has been given a trial in a considerable number of cases, usually in combination with tetanus antitoxin, but the results have been disappointing. The dosage must be considerable and the treatment must be kept up well into convalescence ; in one case a relapse was reported to have followed its abrupt discontinuance. The following strengths of carbolic acid have been recommended.

   i. 20 c. c. doses of a 1 per cent. solution.
   ii. 20 minim ,, ,, 2   ,,   ,,
   iii. 2 c. c.   ,, ,, 5   ,,   ,,

The inoculations are made either subcutaneously or intra-muscularly every 3 or 4 hours, the interval between the doses being lengthened as the spasms diminish in frequency. In no case has any local trouble been reported, nor has carboluria followed even large and frequently repeated doses.

(E.) **Magnesium sulphate.**—Three methods of employing this drug have been advocated. (*a*) The subcutaneous inoculation of doses of 2 c. c. of a 25 per cent solution. (*b*) The subcutaneous inoculation of large quantities of a more dilute solution, Greely recommending the injection of a 1 to 2 per cent solution in quantities varying from 1 pint to 1 quart every 3 hours, according to the severity of the case. (*c*) The intra-thecal method. For this Phillips advises the inoculation of a 25 per cent solution, after withdrawing some of the cerebro-spinal fluid ; 1 c. c. being given for each 25 lbs. of body weight, corresponding to 5 or 6 c. c. for a man of average size. The head of the bed should be propped up after the operation. The advocates of this method claim that it gives relief from pain, controls spasm and ensures sleep. It has been used in this war chiefly by the intra-thecal method, but, like carbolic acid, has not proved reliable.

(F.) **Tetanus antitoxin.**—This is the only treatment as to the employment of which there has been anything like general agreement. It has been used in one form or another in almost every case, and when cure has resulted it has commonly been given the credit. Whatever method be employed it is clear that three general principles must be observed to obtain the best results. It must be employed at the earliest moment possible ; a dose of 1,000–1,500 units given at a time when there is little more than a fear that tetanus may develop, may influence the course of the disease favourably. It must be given in large doses, and these should be frequently repeated until the symptoms show definite signs of amelioration. It must be kept up, although in smaller and less frequent doses, well into convalescence, in order to obviate the tendency to relapse.

The most favourable results appear to have been obtained by the employment, in the first instance, of the intra-thecal combined with the intra-venous methods, the subcutaneous method being used to reinforce the others in the succeeding days, or to replace them as the symptoms diminish in intensity.

Dosage.—An initial intra-thecal dose of 3,000 units followed by the intra-venous injection of doses ranging between 5,000 and 20,000 units, according to the severity of the symptoms, has been reported in many instances to have had a favourable effect. In severe cases, the intra-thecal dose of 3,000 units may be repeated the next day.

The subsequent indications as to dosage depend upon the progress of the case ; if this is favourable the above methods may be supplemented or replaced by the subcutaneous one, doses of from 5,000 to 10,000 units being given every day or every second day.

Anaphylaxis.—Symptoms of this grave condition are well known in animals to follow the administration of a second dose of the same serum when the lapse of time between the two doses exceeds ten or twelve days. There was some reason to fear its occurrence in men who had received a preventive dose of tetanus serum after being wounded, and who, on account of the development of the disease after an interval of twelve days or more, were given therapeutic doses of the same serum. Again, a large number of men who have returned to the front after recovery from a wound are again wounded, and the question has been raised as to the possible danger of giving another preventive dose of serum after an interval of some weeks or months. It is, however, well known that man is much less sensitive to anaphylaxis than the guinea pig and the rabbit, and this has been fully borne out by the experience of this war. In spite of close inquiries on the subject no certain instance of true anaphylaxis has been recorded. The few cases which have been mentioned in reports have, on investigation, turned out to be instances of serum-sickness and to have had no grave results. It does not, therefore, appear to be justifiable to withhold the serum in the case of a man wounded for the second time ; at all events, it appears better to run the small and chiefly theoretical danger of anaphylaxis than the very grave one of tetanus.

In cases in which there is reason to fear the occurrence of anaphylactic shock, various procedures have been recommended to lessen the danger. The majority of these are "fractional" methods of administering the serum, a preliminary inoculation of two or three drops of the serum being given, in dilution, followed in five minutes by a dose of 0·5 c. c. If no untoward symptoms result it is said that the full dose may safely be inoculated ten minutes later. A similar fractional method has been advised if the intravenous or the intra-thecal methods are selected, but there has been no opportunity of judging of their value. Administration of the serum under chloroform anæsthesia is also said to lessen the danger. If symptoms of shock should develop, in spite of these precautions, adrenalin has been stated to be useful, given intra-venously in high dilution if the symptoms are urgent, hypodermically in less urgent conditions in doses of a few minims of a 1–1000 solution.

RECURRENT AND SECONDARY HÆMORRHAGE.

The rules laid down for the treatment of primary hæmorrhage are equally applicable to the recurring variety.

Secondary Hæmorrhage.—The treatment of this accident, which has been painfully prominent by reason of the septic character of a large majority of the wounds, is one of the most difficult problems that has had to be met. The obvious indication, local ligature of the bleeding vessel, may be impracticable for various reasons : (a) the condition of the tissues may be such that a ligature cannot be applied with any hope that it will be permanently efficient ; (b) the position of the bleeding point may render it impossible to apply a ligature. In the former instance it may be necessary to revert to the objectionable process of plugging, and in this case the plug must be retained for a period of at least 48 hours if the bleeding has been severe. In the second instance the

Secondary hæmorrhage.

difficulty may often be surmounted by the application of pressure forceps left in position. The application of a proximal ligature to the main trunk supplying the limb is most undesirable : this practice throughout the whole history of military surgery has been fraught with disaster. Should it prove necessary to ligate a main trunk, the ligature must be placed in the immediate proximity of the wound.

Proximal ligature.

Amputation.—When other means have been exhausted, and provided the general condition of the patient warrants the risk, a recurrence of secondary hæmorrhage should, when practicable, be treated by removal of the limb.

METHODS OF AMPUTATION.

The difficulties attending the performance of amputations during an active campaign form no new experience, since the dangers resulting from the probabilities of infection, and the unfavourable influence of early transport on a recent amputation have been recognized throughout the history of military surgery.

In the present war the great frequency of anaerobic infections, the spread of which is so rapid and disastrous in its results, has greatly increased the difficulties of the problem.

For this reason certain general directions have been formulated below, but it must be understood that when the possibility of performing a *really* " clean operation " exists, the ordinary surgical procedure should not be departed from, although even in that case the provision for drainage must be far more than usually liberal.

Amputations through uninfected tissues.

1. When a primary amputation is indicated by the degree of injury a simple circular or flap amputation so designed as to meet the exigencies of the particular case is suitable. In view of the experience that primary

union is rarely attained such amputations should not be closed by sutures.

Amputations with osteoplastic flaps, the success of which depends upon primary union, or such as Stephen Smith's at the knee joint, should not be performed.

2. Amputations for the removal of limbs of which the tissues are seriously infected either by anaerobic organisms or streptococci should be made either by the circular method with very short flap, and left entirely open ; or, by the flapless method advocated by Lieut. Fitzmaurice Kelly. In cases where the amputation is carried through infected tissues, especially when the infection is anaerobic in nature, the latter method has merits which outweigh the disadvantage that a second operation for the removal of bone may be necessitated. *Amputations through infected tissues.*

(a) The amputation can be done at a lower level, since it may be carried through infected tissues, which latter in consequence of the free drainage provided, may recover. *The flapless method.*

(b) The dangers to the patient of local extension of the infective process, and of systemic infection are minimised.

(c) The section of the soft parts may, without any disadvantage, be made to correspond in level with that of a fracture of the bone.

Extensive use of the method has fully demonstrated these advantages.

Disarticulation, especially through the knee joint, has not proved itself of any material advantage.

CHOICE OF ANÆSTHETIC.

Open ether is the anæsthetic which should generally be adopted when practicable. In patients suffering from septic infections the administration of chloroform is attended with immediate risk, and ulterior bad effects on the general condition of the patient. *Open ether.*

Spinal
anæsthesia.

For major amputations of the lower limbs, spinal
anæsthesia is of great value in minimizing shock,
especially in patients suffering from septicæmia. It must
be borne in mind, however, that the mental shock accompanying these operations is of much importance, especially
in patients whose nervous system has been already
shaken ; for this reason light general anæsthesia during
the introduction of the stovaine should generally be
adopted.

WOUNDS OF THE GREAT VESSELS, AND ANEURYSMS.

It may be premised that any approximately accurate
knowledge as to the number of men who die of primary
hæmorrhage upon the field is still wanting. Any opportunity of affording information on this subject should be
utilized.

Hæmorr-
hage.

Some wounds of the great vessels may be unaccompanied
by considerable primary hæmorrhage; in others a preliminary sharp spurt is followed by spontaneous cessation
of bleeding, which then rarely recurs. In many instances
the main vessel or vessels of the limbs have been completely severed without the causation of any material
hæmorrhage either externally or into the tissues.
Primary ligature of the great trunks is therefore rarely
necessary, and is always undesirable.

Indications
for treat-
ment of
arterial
hæmatoma.

Arterial hæmatoma.—At first a diffuse pulsating
swelling, the blood cavity as a rule tends to become
localised, and a so-called false aneurysm is developed.
This not infrequently becomes consolidated without
surgical treatment.

Early operation is called for only in the circumstances set out below :—

(*a*) Secondary hæmorrhage.

(*b*) Continuous increase in size.

(*c*) Secondary diffusion.

(*d*) When the tumour is large, becomes solid throughout, and gives rise to danger of gangrene from pressure on the collateral vessels.

(*e*) When suppuration threatens.

For an arterial hæmatoma a ligature should be placed on each side of the wound in the vessel, care being taken to close also any branch which may arise opposite the point of injury. *Mode of operation.*

When early operation is required Esmarch's tourniquet is always to be employed if practicable.

If the vessel be the external iliac, it should be remembered that the abdominal aorta may be safely controlled by a long piece of drainage tube tied round the body for a sufficient length of time to perform the operation of ligation.

If a tourniquet be inapplicable, hæmorrhage must be controlled by direct pressure on the wound in the vessel by a finger introduced into the cavity of the hæmatoma.

The most hazardous operations are those at the root of the neck.

Localized false aneurysms rarely need early treatment.

Arterio-venous aneurysms.—In the absence of any of the complications mentioned above, these should be treated expectantly and transferred to England. If operation is imperative, the vessels should be ligatured locally above and below the communication. Proximal ligature of the artery alone has been frequently followed by gangrene of the limb, and is not to be performed. *Arterio-venous aneurysms.*

Aneurysmal varices never need early treatment, and may often be disregarded entirely. *Aneurysmal varices.*

THE TREATMENT OF FRACTURES.

The administration of tetanus anti-toxin and the careful mechanical cleansing of the wounds must be attended to in these as in all other wounds, but the particular difficulty in this group is to determine whether or not the wound must be opened up. Unrestricted drainage is of the highest importance, and in any case of doubt it is better to err on the side of surgical interference.

All fractures caused by gunshot wounds are liable to be complicated by severe laceration of the soft tissues. This is especially the case where the injury is caused by ragged fragments of shell which may tear away large masses of muscle and skin and bruise the tissues to a great depth from the exposed surface. Bullets also, may cause such extensive tearing, that the part looks as if it had "Explosive" been struck by a shell fragment. This is especially the wounds. case when the fracture is due to a bullet fired at very close range, and when the bone struck is a large one, such as the femur or the humerus. In such cases it is the exit wound which is so large and lacerated, and this is due to the fact that the bullet travelling at the height of its velocity, not only smashes the bone, but also imparts its momentum to the shattered fragments and drives them in front of it ; the resulting wound is caused as much by the broken fragments as by the bullet, and the wound is often said to be of the "explosive type." In other cases where the entrance and exit wounds of a bullet are small, there may yet be much tearing of the muscles, and as a result the limb is liable to become much swollen by the subsequent interstitial bleeding. In this event it is most important to remove the dressings first applied as soon as possible, and never in any circumstances to bandage the limb without first putting on a splint and a large quantity of cotton wool. Much harm is often done by bandages applied tightly over first field dressings by the comrades of the patient, and care should be taken at field ambulances and clearing stations to see that bandages have not become too tight owing to the swelling of the limb. *Tight bandaging of fractures.*

A triangular bandage is often better than the roller applied spirally.

TREATMENT OF THE WOUND.

A.—Fractures caused by rifle bullets, in which the entrance and exit wounds are quite small, and there is no great extravasation of blood along the bullet track are the only cases in which it is safe to rely merely upon the cleansing of the external wounds. All other cases should be investigated under an anæsthetic as early as possible. *Simple bullet wounds.*

B.—Fractures caused by rifle bullets in which there is a small entrance wound, and an exit wound of the "explosive type," call for an exploration under an anæsthetic in order to remove blood-clot, fragments of clothing, dirt, or completely detached portions of bone. This removal is better done under the eye by using retractors, and not by mopping the wound out through an insufficient opening. Flushing by a stream of fluid from a large irrigator is advisable at the end of the operation. In the first instance, at any rate, no fragments of bone should be removed unless they are completely detached. Badly bruised and devitalized tissues should be cut away, and the edges of the skin wound cleanly excised. *Severe bullet wounds.* *Removal of fragments.*

When the wound has been thoroughly cleansed, provision must be made for efficient drainage. In the *Drainage.*

cases under consideration the existing wounds will generally be sufficient for the purpose. One or more large sized drainage tubes should be used (from $\frac{1}{2}$ to $\frac{3}{4}$ inch in diameter), and these may be passed through from one wound to another or inserted at each opening.

No tube should be passed across a limb so as to traverse the defect in the bone, neither should it lie in close proximity to a large vessel. In no circumstances should the wound be tightly packed with gauze. Gauze wicks should never be used instead of tubes. The question of dressings is treated separately. (*See* p. 5 *et seq.*)

Few methods of treatment have proved more satisfactory at the base for this type of case, than that of continuous irrigation.

Shell wounds.

C.—Fractures caused by fragments of shell or the irregular impact of ricochet or deflected bullets require the most careful attention. Very free drainage, in addition to thorough cleansing of the superficial wounds, is most essential, as wounds of this type are especially apt to be followed by the development of gas-gangrene.

Drainage.

In order to ensure drainage the skin wounds must if necessary be freely enlarged, and some portion of the herniated muscle that so often blocks the opening may have to be cut away. This should be done the more freely when the herniated mass is black and gangrenous.

When only a wound of entry exists, the skin must be incised freely. All clot and foreign material must be removed, and efficient drainage secured by means of large tubes inserted through one or more counter-openings so placed as to ensure the drainage of the entire cavity. It is advisable that no fractures of this type should be sent to the base until this has been done.

TREATMENT OF SOME SPECIAL FRACTURES.*

A.—**Of the Humerus.**—At field ambulances and clear- Fractures of
ing stations these fractures are often best treated by the arm at
applying short wooden splints and bandaging the arm to bulances.
the chest so that the whole limb is steadied during
transit by ambulance wagon and rail.

In nearly all these cases treated in bed at base hospitals At the base.
a fixation apparatus should be used that provides a constantly acting extention and does not need to be removed
for the purpose of renewing dressings. The simplest
apparatus possessing these advantages is probably
Thomas's knee splint, which may be suspended in the
abducted position to the suspension rail of a Balkan
splint or any similar upright.

Patients able to walk may be put up in a splint of
the type of Robert Jones's modification of Thomas's knee
splint, Fig. 6 (p. 33), or a Strohmeyer's cushion may be
employed.

Methods of direct mechanical fixation should not be
used.

B.—**Of the Femur.**—The same principles apply to these Fractures
fractures as apply to those of the humerus, but the of the
difficulty in applying them is much greater. thigh.

In the first instance, and for the purpose of transit,
one of the modifications of Thomas's splint described
below, or a long outside splint with a bracketted inter-
ruption opposite the wound, may be employed.

As much extension as possible should be made while
the patient is under the anæsthetic, and the splint is
being put on.

---

* See Appendix as to mode of application of the splints referred to
(p. 35).

For use at the base hospitals some form of splint is required that will keep up a constantly acting extension. This is most important, not only in order to maintain the functional power of the limb, but to avoid mobility of the fractured ends, which, if unchecked, may lead to extension of sepsis, swelling of the limb from pressure upon the vessels, and secondary hæmorrhage.

The following methods have proved themselves the most useful out of the very large number tried during the present campaign :—

Types of splint for lower ⅓ of bone.

(*a*) Thomas's knee splint, or one of its modifications (see Appendix, p. 35), is very useful and comfortable in cases of fracture below the junction of the upper with the middle third of the femur.

For upper ⅓.

(*b*) For fractures of the upper third, the abduction frame of Robert Jones is often useful, or Wallace's splint, or one of the next two forms of apparatus may be employed.

(*c*) The Balkan Splint has been widely used. Its chief defect lies in the difficulty of maintaining sufficiently powerful extension. It is, however, very comfortable and convenient for temporary use, as ready access to the wound can always be obtained. The slings for the thigh can be reinforced by a posterior dish splint made of wire or perforated zinc, which if necessary can be provided with an opening opposite the wound.

(*d*) Hodgen's wire suspension splint is an excellent apparatus, but it needs constant attention and readjustment ; hence, it is not so popular as its merits deserve.

Warning as to use of perineal band.

(*e*) If a " Long Liston " or any of its modifications is used, a perineal band should not be employed for patients coming down from the field ambulances or

FIG. 1.—Skeleton splint for fractures of the leg or injuries near the ankle joint.

FIG. 1A.—The " Boulogne box." Two long outside splints united, at the foot, by two cross ties beneath the lower extremities, and an iron hoop across the chest. The trunk is supported by a broad canvas sling attached to the upper part of the splint.

clearing stations. It has been found to cause considerable swelling of the thigh, and by the pressure exercised to favour the extension of anaerobic infections.

(*f*) If the splint already in use is suitable for travelling, no change need be made for transportation to England. If extension is not essential the "Boulogne Box" has proved very satisfactory (Fig. 1A). A bracketted Long Liston is comfortable, not cumbrous, and some extension can be maintained by means of it.

Splints for use during transportation.

C. **Of the Tibia and Fibula.**—A back splint with foot piece and side splints is as comfortable and efficient as any if there is no wound in the calf. Either a Thomas's knee splint, that of Robert Jones (Fig. 1), or a Balkan splint will give good results in other cases, as all allow free access for dressing without the necessity for removing the splint.

Fractures of the leg.

OPERATIVE TREATMENT OF COMPOUND FRACTURES.

It is best not to use wires or plates or any other form of direct mechanical fixation. In every septic wound necrosis and further spread of infection are easily caused, and screws and rivets rapidly become loose in suppurating wounds.

Direct mechanical fixation.

Comminuted Fractures involving the Great Joints.— Some of these are only suitable for amputation. In the case of fine comminution of the head of the femur or humerus, the fragments may occasionally be advantageously removed primarily and a modified excision of the joint effected. In the case of the elbow joint similar primary operations may also be considered. These operations are suitable where the other bone or bones forming the joint are intact.

Fractures involving joints.

Amputation will be called for as a *primary* measure when the limb is hopelessly shattered, when it is gangrenous, or when the case is not seen until advanced gas-gangrene has set in.

In some of these last cases the patient's condition may be too bad to warrant the performance of an immediate amputation, and free incisions must then be made in the hope of clearing up the infection sufficiently to permit of the amputation being performed as a secondary measure. In primary amputation of the thigh the injection of stovaine either into the spinal canal, or into the limb so as to block the main nerve paths may be very beneficial.

Amputation as a *secondary* measure will be called for in cases running an unfavourable course. The indications for amputation here are the same as those prevailing in similar cases not due to gunshot injuries.

Transference to England.— The question of the time at which cases of compound fracture should be transferred to England is of importance. On the whole, perhaps, the best rule to lay down is that transfer may be effected as soon as the wound is draining thoroughly, and the temperature chart is satisfactory. In time of stress, patients who are well enough may be transferred immediately they have been drained efficiently.

To face p. 35.

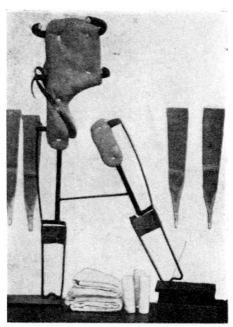

FIG. 3.—R. Jones's abduction frame modified for use in cases of pelvic or gluteal wound.

To face p. 35.

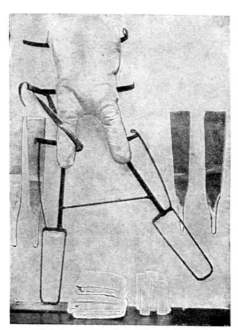

FIG. 2.—Left abduction frame, with adhesive strapping extension bands, wool and bandages used in its application.

Appendix on the application of certain Splints.*

FRACTURES OF THE LOWER LIMB.

Hip and Upper Thigh.—The abduction frame is a splint upon which the patient lies and can be carried. Extension is easily maintained and applied, and need not be relaxed for any purpose. (Figs. 2 and 3.) *R. Jones's Abduction frame.*

The patient is placed upon this splint, and any displacement should be overcome by immediate extension in the abducted plane.

The limb should be rotated inwards slightly until the foot is at right angles to the table, and be fixed in this position on the frame.

Both limbs are controlled, and extension secured by strapping applied to the injured limb; counter extension is effected by means of a small leather groin strap on the opposite side of the pelvis. This groin strap should not be slackened under any pretext, but in order to avoid pressure sores, the nurse should be instructed to alter the area of the skin over the adductors which is subjected to pressure, by moving it to and fro.

Upper, Middle, and Lower Thigh.—The application of the Thomas knee splint is quite easy. Strapping of adhesive plaster is applied in the usual way to the sides of the limb. At the lower end of the extension strapping there is a loop of webbing to which is attached a length of strong bandage. The ring of the splint is passed over the foot, and up the groin until it is firmly against the tuber ischii. (Figs. 4 and 5.) *Thomas's knee splint.*

---

* These directions are quoted from papers by Major Robert Jones, *Brit. Med. Jour.*, Jan. 16th, 1915; Colonel C. S. Wallace, *Lancet*, Feb. 13th, 1915, and Captain Max Page, *Brit. Med. Jour.*, May 15th, 1915.

The extensions are then pulled tight, the ends turned round each side bar and tied together over the bottom end of the splint, which should project 6 or 8 inches beyond the foot. Care must be taken to avoid internal or external rotation of the limb, the foot being kept at right angles.

Local splints can then be employed if needed ; these are made of perforated zinc, block tin, or sheet iron. They can be moulded by the hand to fit the limb, and yet, being gutter-shaped, they are rigid longitudinally. They can be disinfected by fire or water. A couple of transverse bandage slings suspend the limb from the side bars of the knee splint. A straight splint is placed behind the suspensory bandages of the thigh and knee. On the front of the thigh another sheet-iron splint is applied, and the femur is thus kept rigid.

The alignment from the hip joint to the ankle is perfect, being dependent on a straight pull.

In using this splint a little attention is necessary to prevent soreness of the perineum. The ring of the splint, being covered with smooth basil leather, can easily be kept clean, so can the skin. The nurse should also several times a day press down the skin of the buttock and draw a fresh part of the skin under the splint. To change the point of pressure over the perineum the limb can be elevated or abducted. The dressings can be applied without in any way interfering with the work of the splint. When the fracture has occurred through the knee or upper tibia the splint is applied in the same way.

Arm.—Fractures of the middle and lower middle portions of the shaft of the humerus, where dressings have to be frequently changed, require very gentle handling.

Fractures of the arm.

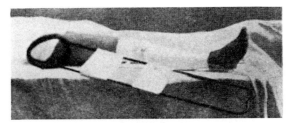

FIG. 4.—Thomas's knee splint ready for application to a
fractured thigh.

FIG. 5.—Thomas's knee splint applied, with the addition of local splints
to the thigh.

FIG. 5A.—The "Balkan support." A Thomas's knee splint applied and suspended to a railroad pulley. The use of the bar of the support in allowing the patient to move himself in bed is also shown.

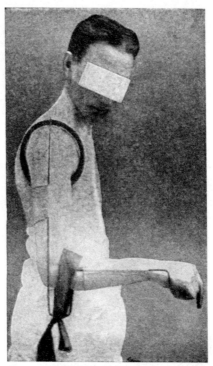

FIG. 6.—Modified Thomas's knee splint for use as a
humerus extension splint.

Two splints may be found very useful.

One is a modified Thomas knee splint used to maintain extension in the abducted position, the patient being recumbent.

The other is a modified Thomas humerus extension splint, to be used when the patient can walk about or sit up in bed. (Fig. 6.)

Either splint permits of easy dressing, and maintains adequate fixation. As so much destruction of bone may be produced by modern shrapnel, and even by rifle bullets, great care must be taken to prevent over extension, otherwise non-union will ensue.

Forearm.—In dealing with these fractures, whether one or more bones be broken, the position of supination should invariably be maintained. This is even more important in septic compound fractures than where no complication exists. Fractures of the forearm.

Neglect of this important point will often result in a locking of the bones in pronation.

Wrist and Hand.—In order that the fingers may maintain their grasping power, injuries of the wrist joint should be treated in the dorsiflexed position (*Brit. Med. Journ.*, Jan. 16th, 1915). (Fig. 7.)

It must however be borne in mind that prolonged extension of the wrist in a position of dorsiflexion may cause undesirable stretching of the flexor muscles, hence it is necessary to exercise vigilance in employing this splint.

Wallace's Splint.—A modification of Thomas's knee splint devised by Col. Cuthbert Wallace and Capt. Maybury, as affording the greatest possibilities for extension, is very useful in the base hospitals. (Fig. 8.) Wallace's splint.

The process of application is as follows :—The ring is slipped over the foot and adjusted in the ordinary way, Mode of application.

care being taken that the inner and back part of the ring gets a bearing on the tuber ischii. As the ring is rather large, this is ensured by putting a pad on the outer side of the thigh. The foot is then fastened to the footpiece by a stirrup extension or a leather anklet, or by webbing embedded in plaster put on over wool wrapped round foot and ankle. The limb is supported in the splint by the two parallel bars in the same way that is usual in the Hodgen splint. The lower transverse sliding piece is then fixed to the two parallel bars by screws provided for the purpose, and extension applied to the limb by turning the traction screw. The end of the splint is either rested on sandbags, supported by the prop of Page's splint, or swung by a chain from a masthead or from the roof of the hut (Fig. 9). By this means the patient is free to move about in bed within reasonable limits, and the dressing of a posterior wound can be effected without discomfort to the patient by either raising the splint or turning him on one side, the constant steady pull of the screw preventing any undue shifting of the limb and consequent pain to the patient. If the limb tends to sag when the patient is turned on his side it can be prevented by loops of bandage fastened across the front of the limb.

Use of the pin.

In those cases in which it is impossible to apply the stirrup extension, either because of the state of the skin or from the presence of wounds in the leg, a pin can be driven through the lower end of the femur and the extension applied by a chain or thick picture wire, which runs from one of the ends of the pin down to the transverse footpiece over two pulleys let into this, and up again to the opposite end of the pin.

The use of the pulleys is to allow the strain on either side of the limb to be equal, which is difficult to ensure

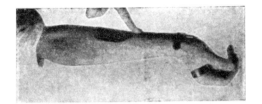

Fig. 7.— Dorsiflexion splint in position.

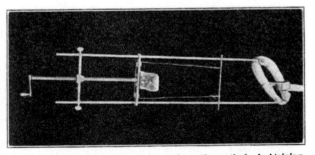

Fig. 8.—Wallace's splint. The diagram shows the method of obtaining extension by means of a transfixion pin. Note the passage of the wire through the pulleys. The traction screw is longer than that now used.

To face p. 39.

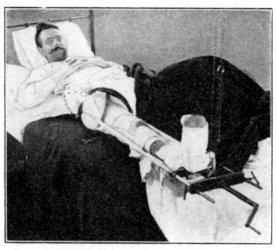

Fig. 9.—Wallace's splint applied to a fractured thigh. The splint is suspended from the roof of a hut by a chain.

if the ends of the pin are fastened to the corresponding ends of the transverse footpiece.

The distance between the parallel bars ensures the easy application of the dressing. If time permits the splint is best applied upon an X-ray table, when by use of the screen, extension can be exercised under an anæsthetic until the alignment of the fragments is good. The essential part of the splint is the screw, and no other method which has been tried produces a like amount of extension with so little discomfort to the patient (*Lancet*, Feb. 13th, 1915).

Page's Splint is founded on the same principle; it is light, well suited for patients subjected to transport and possesses the advantage of being readily made up from the aluminium strips in the field fracture box. *Page's splint.*

Preparation of the Splint.—The measurements required are (*a*) from the tuber ischii to the point of the heel; (*b*) an oblique from the tendon of the adductor longus an inch below its origin, passing behind the limb, to the upper margin of the great trochanter of the femur. The splint is made from two U-shaped pieces of aluminium splinting as usually supplied (length 60 inches). The convexity of one U is bent to form the upper hip crutch, which will be the size of the measurement *b*. *Preparation of the aluminium strips.*

To the lower part of the splint a prop is attached as shown in Fig. 10. This is essential if the splint is to be used for the transport of cases. It keeps the limb even on the splint. The prop can be bent to suit the slope of the stretcher.

For manipulating the splinting a large screw wrench (as supplied with the wheeled stretcher carriages) will be found most useful. The other piece of aluminium band is bent symmetrically to form a stirrup. This stirrup should be formed with a slight concavity downwards in order to keep the extension strap in place. The crutch of the upper U is padded with tow and covered with jaconet. When the splint is wanted, the two U sections are joined together with aluminium ribbon so as to give a length from the margin of the crutch to the stirrup of 4 to 6 inches more than the measurement.—Slings of flannel or other firm material are then attached to the lateral bars of the splint at such levels as to support the limb but not to interfere with the dressings. Fixation of the slings is effected by safety pins.

Mode of application.

Application of the Splint.—To simplify the application of the apparatus, the extension stirrup may be fixed to a leather or soft canvas anklet, which can be buckled on in a few seconds. The splint is then slipped under the leg, and the crutch is moulded to fit the thigh firmly at the upper level, and then fixed by buckle and webbing passing across in front of the limb. Extension is then applied by a strap passed from the loop and round the stirrup.

The slings are passed under the leg and made fast to the outer bar of the splint with safety pins in such a way that the limb lies evenly in the middle of the splint. The extension is then tightened up, and a few straps are applied over the anterior surface to keep the limb firm at times when the patient may be rolled on his side. If the position of the fragments should render some flexion at the knee and hip joints desirable, the splint can be bent into a form like a Hodgen. The self-contained extension will still operate to a sufficient degree. (Fig. 11.)

Modification for the arm in patients confined to bed.

The Thigh Splint modified for the Arm.—A small edition of the femur splint is suitable for many cases of fracture of the arm, especially for those in which frequent dressing of large wounds is called for. The crutch should measure about 5 inches and be bent to form about two-fifths of a circle.

To face p. 40.

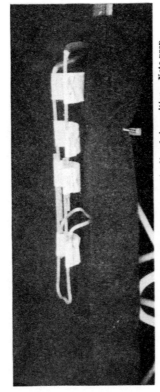

Fig. 10.—Page's thigh splint with supporting bands in position. Note prop beneath leg for the support of the limb when the patient is on a stretcher or in bed.

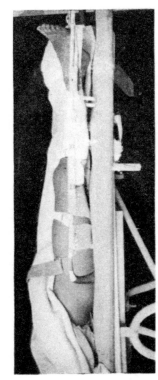

Fig. 11.—Page's thigh splint applied. Note strap across groin and bands crossing the thigh and leg to support the limb when the patient requires to be rolled over in bed.

To face p. 40.

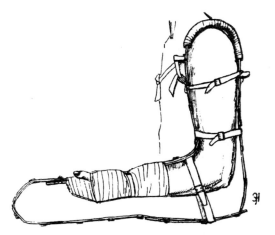

Fig. 12.—Page's flexed arm splint applied. The prolongation beyond
the hand is only of use in those cases of fracture of the
bones of the forearm where extension is required.

The prop is applied at about the centre of the splint. Adhesive extension strips are fixed to the wrist and hand. For transport it will be found that the arm can be comfortably brought down parallel to the trunk. The prop is bent so as to keep the splint level in relation to the stretcher.

The Flexed Arm Splint.—This splint is adapted for the treatment of fractures of the lower two-thirds of the humerus, injuries of the elbow and fractures of the forearm. (Fig. 12.)

It is made from one full-length piece of aluminium, and is completed by a short piece.

This type is suitable for either side, and for any fracture below the upper third of the humerus.

The projection beyond the hand is only wanted for applying extension in forearm cases.

The shoulder arch of the splint may be padded by slipping a stout piece of rubber tubing over it. Rubber tubing covers in the same way the axillary strap, which is attached to two rings made of aluminium ribbon. This strap bears on the two axillary folds, and exerts no pressure on the vessels.

The pad for the hand is fixed to the upper limb of the splint if it is desired to put the arm up in supination, to the lower if in the prone position.

For fractures of the humerus long axis extension is obtained as follows :—After the shoulder piece has been strapped in place the hand is fixed to its pad, traction just below the elbow to the lower band of the splint is made by a belt of webbing or elastic ; a short length of Martin's bandage is useful.

Flexed arm splint.

A piece of composition splinting as supplied in the field fracture box is useful if placed on the upper surface of the forearm in order to distribute the pressure (*Brit. Med. Journ.*, May 15th, 1915).

N.B.—Any of the splints referred to above, or models of them, may be obtained from the Base Medical Stores.

TREATMENT OF WOUNDS OF JOINTS.

Wounds of the knee-joint are more frequent and liable to be more disastrous in their consequences than those of any other joint. Their treatment, therefore, will be indicated, and the principles advocated can be adapted for other joints.

Nature of the injuries. The nature of the injuries and the infection, coupled with the unfavourable conditions under which the wound is received and the impossibility which may exist of giving adequate attention to such injuries in the early stages, frequently give rise to such an exceedingly rapid inflammatory disintegration of the joint and breakdown of the patient's general resistance that amputation is the only means of saving the patient's life. Later, one must not be tempted, on account of the apparently quiescent and fairly painless condition of the joint in certain cases, to postpone radical operation very long. In consequence of the communication of the wound in the bone or joint with the exterior, symptoms due to increased tension in the part are absent, and therefore the ordinarily described type of osteomyelitis or arthritis is not usually found. Patients with such injuries usually have an obstinately high temperature, and if the cause of this and of the steady, but probably insidious, deterioration in the general condition is not attributable to some other cause, amputation must be done.

Certain common types of injury may be summarised :— Types of injury.

(1) *Cases of effusion without lodgment of the projectile in the joint.*—(*a*) In which it is uncertain whether the synovial cavity has been traversed or the synovial membrane has been merely bruised. (*b*) In which the synovial cavity has been traversed by a clean rifle bullet without injury to the bones. (*c*) In which the bullet has cleanly perforated one of the bones, entering into the articulation.

In connection with injuries of this class the common association of effusion into an intact knee-joint with a fracture of the shaft of the femur is to be borne in mind.

Cases included in Class I are obviously subjects for expectant treatment. If suspicion as to infection arises the joint should be tapped and the effusion of blood or synovia examined bacteriologically.

(2) *Cases in which the projectile has lodged* (*a*) within the synovial cavity, and (*b*) in one of the articular ends. Retained missiles.

When a retained rifle bullet lies within the joint, if the superficial wound is small and not inflamed, it may usually be left with safety until firm union of the primary track has occurred.

Free fragments of shells or bombs or distorted rifle bullets must be promptly removed.

Bullets or shell fragments embedded in the articular ends of the long bones form a difficult problem. Clean rifle bullets so situated as not to interfere with the move- Missiles embedded in the bones.

ments of the joint should certainly not be interfered with at an early stage. They may do no harm and have frequently been left indefinitely. Fragments of shells come into a different category. Here infective material has practically always been carried in and the retained body must be removed by the shortest and safest route. This may be by the original wound, although sometimes the localising skiagrams may indicate a much shorter route, but as the bed of the missile is certainly infected, no advantage except that of direct access is gained by a special incision. As the extraction is commonly a matter of considerable difficulty the incision for the removal of impacted bodies should be free, and it is well to remove any of the bone surrounding the fragment which may have become infected. One or more tablets of salt may be placed in the cavity in the bone. A tube should be inserted directly into the aperture of the bone defect. This should be packed around with gauze wet with 5 per cent saline solution, and the limb fixed on a splint. The packing is renewed daily, if necessary, for three or four days, in the hope of confining the extent of the infection to the region of the injury to the bone.

Open wounds of the joint.

3. *Cases in which the synovial cavity has been more or less widely opened* (a) without damage to the articular surfaces, and (b) where fissured fracture or slight comminution of the articular ends of the bones coexists.

Flesh wounds involving the synovial cavity and injuries in which fissuring or local comminution of the articular ends of the bones exist in connection with an external wound require the primary measures which are detailed later on. Careful treatment of the wound and immobilisation of the joint may sometimes be followed by sealing of the opening in the synovial membrane by the formation of local adhesions, but drainage of the joint is often called for at a slightly later period.

(4) *Cases in which serious comminution of one or more of the constituent bones has occurred.*

The majority of cases in which gross comminution of either femur or tibia is present eventually require amputation. Severe compound T-shaped fractures of the lower end of the femur can rarely be saved and primary amputation is frequently advisable. Extensive comminution of the cancellous tissue of the head of the tibia may prove very dangerous owing to the severe constitutional symptoms which follow septic absorption from the injured spongy bone. Treatment with strong hypertonic saline solution tends to prevent the occurrence of this complication. *[side note: Seriously comminuted fractures.]*

Comminuted fractures of the patella form a special class. The loose fragments, sometimes amounting to the entire bone, should be removed. It is sometimes possible to close the hole thus made by suture of the synovial membrane and make an attempt to obtain a movable joint, but usually free lateral incisions made at the most dependent portions of the synovial reflexions are necessary. *[side note: Fractures of the patella.]*

This recommendation does not refer to cases in which an ordinary transverse fracture of the patella has been produced by a sudden muscular contraction following a bullet wound of the thigh, even though the bullet should have traversed the knee-joint. Neither should it be extended to clean fractures of the bone even if produced by direct passage of the bullet.

TREATMENT AT THE FRONT.

Generally speaking, if the joint is extensively shattered and soiled, especially if the main vessels or nerves are torn, primary amputation must be done. Fractures which radiate to the medullary cavity of the femur or tibia may, later on, prove especially dangerous.

Mere comminution of the condyles or of the head of the tibia does not necessarily indicate operation. In many of these cases and in the majority of other wounds of the knee, no operative treatment should be undertaken until the patient reaches a hospital where he can be retained for at least seven to fourteen days after operation. Primary efforts should be confined to effecting thorough disinfection of the surrounding skin, removal of visible or palpable foreign bodies, and adequate fixation of the joint. No drainage tubing should be inserted into the joint at this stage.

Movements of the joint may turn the scale in favour of extension of sepsis and may make all the difference to the patient's future. Therefore, all cases in which the synovial membrane is wounded, however trivial the injury may appear to be, should be fixed comfortably in a splint in a position of slight flexion. One of the best splints for the less severe cases at this time is the gutter "fracture splint," recommended by Major Robert Jones, which can easily be bent to the shape required. It should reach from below the ischial tuberosity to the heel.

In the worst cases one of the splints recommended for fracture of the thigh should be used; on no account should a short splint be applied. Dressings must not be bandaged on so firmly as to interfere with exudation, either from the joint or superficial wound.

TREATMENT AT THE BASE.

On admission of the patient, the skin around the wound, and for 6 to 8 inches above and below the knee, should be shaved and disinfected and a dressing applied to this area. The joint should be immobilized in a position most comfortable to the patient, usually in slight flexion. The modified Thomas's knee splint or Wallace's splint, in which "self-contained extension" can be made, is probably best for this purpose. The knee should be supported by a slightly bent metal or other gutter splint of suitable length. The Thomas's splint can often be kept in position until cure is effected. If necessary, the lateral bars can be bent outward opposite the knee to allow free access to the wound.

An X-ray picture should be taken, to ascertain the presence and position of foreign bodies, or the extent of bony injuries. In the absence of a localiser, skiagrams in planes at right angles to each other must be made.

Treatment of the superficial wound.—If suppuration is present, the wound should be opened up freely and all foreign material removed. Necrotic tissue should be cut away, or better still, if possible, the whole wound should be excised *en masse*. Sutures should not be introduced so as in any way to impair free drainage.

This treatment should be carried out even though the wound does not communicate with the joint, otherwise infection may spread through the bruised tissues into the joint. Strong antiseptics should not be used, as they may cause necrosis of the damaged tissues. Hypertonic saline dressings are probably best in such circumstances, and should be left as long as possible without being changed. Rough removal of adherent dressings may open the joint. When dressings *are* adherent it is usually unnecessary to remove them. A drainage tube should always be placed in the dressings to conduct away discharge from the depth of the wound or from the opening in the synovial membrane.

Treatment of effusion.—High temperature accompanying effusion in the early days does not necessarily mean a septic joint. When effusion is present, if there is doubt as to infection, or if there is great tension in the joint, a large exploring or aspirating needle should be introduced to relieve the tension, and give the opportunity for bacteriological examination of the fluid.

Aspiration.

If the effusion is sterile the joint must be kept at rest until danger of infection from the superficial wound is past. If the fluid re-accumulates to a marked extent, the aspiration is repeated. If after aspiration there is much pain in the joint, slight extension, applied to the leg, will probably give relief.

If the effusion is infected, it should be aspirated as completely as possible, and extension should be applied to the distal part of the limb so as to relieve the compression of the articular cartilages caused by muscular spasm. Unless extension is made, erosion of the cartilage may occur very quickly. Before withdrawing the aspirating needle, it is advisable to inject formalin-glycerin, iodoform-ether, or ether. Two drachms of 2 per cent formalin in glycerin, prepared not less than 12 hours or more than one week previously. Two to four drachms iodoform-ether (10–20 grs. to 1 oz.) or a similar quantity of ether. The injections should be repeated every 2–6 days. It is difficult at present to state which preparation is the best, but formalin-glycerin and plain ether are those most often used. In a case which is improving the injections must be continued until organisms are no longer found in the effusion. The same course should be followed even if organisms be found which do not grow on culture media. In some cases 5 per cent saline solution has been successful. During all this time immobilisation of the joint must be strictly preserved.

Injection of antiseptics.

If the effusion continues to accumulate but remains mildly septic, effusion being the main feature in the absence of pyrexia or serious local inflammatory signs, the following course may be taken. A large aspirating needle or canula is inserted at either side of the joint cavity. One is connected with a reservoir of hypertonic (5 per cent) salt solution, and the other with a receptacle at the side of the bed. Care must be taken that no air enters the joint during the procedure, and irrigation may be kept up for 24 hours, at the end of which time the needles are withdrawn. The effect of this procedure is to wash away the pus which has collected in the anterior parts of the joint, while by the diffusion of the hypertonic solution lymph lavage of the posterior parts is stimulated. *Continuous irrigation.*

If mild sepsis still persists, cure has been obtained by the introduction of a tube just above the patella, from one side to the other. The joint is opened through vertical incisions running parallel to the margin of each condyle and thoroughly washed out with 5 per cent saline solution before introducing the tube. The tube must not be left in the joint for longer than two days, otherwise such dense adhesions are formed that mobility may be permanently impaired. *Temporary tube drainage.*

The method described above may lead to the cure of what, on admission, appeared to be a fulminating arthritis, or may transform the arthritis into one of a mild type. If, in spite of these procedures, acute inflammation persists, the joint must be freely laid open.

If the presence of much infected clot in the synovial cavity is suspected, it is better to open the joint freely through unbroken skin, and wash out the clot. The joint is then again closed, and one of the antiseptic solutions recommended above is injected, the limb being put up as already described, *Infected clot.*

If the wound has implicated the synovial membrane *so that the joint is actually open*, success may still be obtained, even though fairly active suppuration is present. The superficial part of the wound is dealt with as already described, the ragged, soiled edges of the synovial membrane are cut away, any foreign body present is removed, the synovial cavity is washed out with saline solution, and the joint is treated as before, except that the synovial membrane is not sutured. The dressings of the superficial wound should not be disturbed if possible for several days, during which time a small drainage tube may be left in the dressings to conduct away any fluid exuding from the wound in the synovial membrane. This tube should not project into the joint cavity.

If in such a case the infection is very severe, absolutely free drainage must be established. This is most difficult to obtain without sacrificing the future efficiency of the joint. If a fracture exists and pocketing of pus has also developed, ankylosis is the best result to be hoped for. Pus has a most marked tendency to burrow in these cases, especially into the back of the thigh and calf. The strain on the general health of the patient may be intense, while secondary troubles, such as septicæmia, pyæmia, and secondary hæmorrhage are peculiarly liable to develop.

Methods of drainage.—1. The joint is opened by incisions in the long axis of the limb, extending the entire length of the lateral reflexions of the synovial membrane at its most dependent level. These incisions are best made by opening the large pouch of the joint above and then continuing the incision downwards close to the line of reflexion of the synovial membrane from the bones. If necessary, at a later date, the lower extremities of the two lateral incisions may be connected, and a flap thus raised which will expose the whole interior of the joint,

When the joint cavity has been thoroughly flushed,
drainage tubes may be inserted, if it be wished to
use continuous irrigation. Another method consists in
packing the synovial cavity with gauze. The latter
requires to be replaced daily. For the first two days an
anæsthetic is required for this purpose ; after these two
dressings no anæsthetic should be necessary. The packing holds apart the synovial surfaces, thus preventing
primary adhesion between them, and further, the gauze,
by capillary action, sucks up discharge from the deeper
recesses of the joint. The process of packing may require
to be continued for a week or more.

2. The joint is opened by a single transverse subpatellar *Drainage*
anterior incision. This incision may be used for the *by sub-*
worst type of case, where ankylosis is the object, and it *patellar*
is thought that amputation may possibly be avoided. *incision.*

The incision should extend so far on each side that no
deep recesses are left posteriorly ; the lateral ligaments
are freely divided. The crucial ligaments are cut across
and the semi-lunar cartilages removed. The opposing
articular surfaces are then easily drawn apart to allow
free access to the posterior part of the joint.

Any communicating pockets of pus should be freely
laid open and drained. It is advisable in most cases to
remove shattered pieces of the articular ends of the bone.
These are apt to necrose, and inflammation is prone to
spread up or down the crevices and lead to osteomyelitis
of the femur or tibia. Their removal may greatly
facilitate drainage. The exposed parts may now be
dressed with any of the usual antiseptic dressings, but
some surgeons strongly advocate the following dressing
for this as well as for other wounds.

Tablets of sodium chloride and sodium citrate may
be placed in all pockets and in crevices in the bone,

as well as in the folds of gauze saturated in strong hypertonic solution, which are now carefully and fairly firmly packed around the ends of the bones and into any large pockets. A large tube, for drainage of the central parts and for the introduction of more tablets into lumen if thought necessary, is placed amongst the folds of gauze. Any posterior synovial pouches should be drained. No suturing is done. These dressings may often be left for several days at a time. Only the superficial layers of gauze and wool on the skin need be changed.

The knee is placed afterwards on its outer side, on a pillow or special splint, in strong flexion or else in a straight splint with slight extension applied to the leg so that the articular surfaces are separated freely. Care must be taken that the main vessels do not become kinked, or too much pulled upon.

When the raw surfaces are covered with healthy granulations the knee is fixed by suitable splints in a position of very slight flexion. It is necessary first to remove the loosened articular cartilages. A soft drain (e.g., folded jaconet or batiste) should be inserted behind the condyles for a few days.

Whatever method of drainage is employed in these septic cases, particular attention should be given to the synovial pouches at the back of the joint, especially to the bursa of the popliteus. Infection of this bursa is probably the cause in most cases of the deep suppuration which tracks down into the calf, and if it be drained by a tube which also drains the posterior part of the knee such abscess formation will probably be prevented. The affected leg in such cases may not be painful and may look normal, or it may appear to be unusually well formed and well-nourished when compared with the other, usually emaciated, leg.

Primary amputation is strongly indicated when comminuted fracture of the articular ends of the bones exists, especially if the fracture implicates the medullary cavities of the bones ; also in cases of serious injury to the main vessels and nerves.

Secondary amputation is indicated in many cases if serious infection attacks the joint, if suppuration persists, if osteomyelitis spreads, if secondary hæmorrhage occurs, or if the patient's general condition deteriorates.

In both cases a simple circular amputation should be made. The stump is left unsutured in acute cases, but in later cases, when sepsis has abated, this procedure can be modified.

SPECIAL REMARKS ABOUT OTHER JOINTS.

Shoulder joint.—If the articular surfaces are shattered, primary excision, with free drainage, preferably posterior, should be carried out. Amputation is not often necessary. If ankylosis is likely to result from the injury, the arm should be fixed in the abducted position.

Elbow joint.—Primary excision is advisable in some severe cases when the bones are shattered. Those cases in which one or other of the bones remain intact are the most favourable. Incisions are planned according to the position of the wounds.

Wrist joint.—Excision of the shattered carpal or adjacent bones is frequently advisable. Very free drainage must be provided. Under the more recent modifications of "hypertonic" saline treatment, amputation is rendered much less frequent. In all cases it is preferable to place the forearm and hand in a splint which holds the hand in dorsiflexion. If ankylosis at the wrist occurs in this position, the functions and power of the hand and fingers are better preserved than they are in any other.

Hip joint.—Free posterior drainage, with fixation in a suitable abduction frame, will succeed in most cases. Excision is occasionally and amputation only rarely advisable.

Ankle joint and tarsal joints.—If the injury is severe or if the infection does not yield readily to free incision and drainage, amputation should be performed without hesitation. The safety assured by the removal of the infected limb, and the art of the artificial-limb maker adequately compensate for the loss of the foot.

TREATMENT OF HEAD INJURIES.

The treatment of gunshot wounds of the head, like that of wounds elsewhere, has to be modified in accordance with existing conditions.

The suggestions made in this memorandum have reference less to the line of treatment which might be followed in ideal circumstances than to that which experience has shown to yield the best results in the actual and varying conditions in which these cases have to be dealt with. Complete and efficient early operation, however desirable, demands more time, material, and assistance than are always available near the front, particularly during a rush of work. In the early part of the war it was found that many cases which had been submitted to operation, performed in unfavourable circumstances and during times of stress, reached the base in a less satisfactory condition for further treatment than if they had been dealt with on more conservative lines.

The difficulties attending early operation at the front are increased by the impossibility of deciding immediately, and without repeated and detailed observation, which are the cases requiring operation. In some the need is clear and imperative; in others it may be equally obvious that no immediate operation is required. In the very large intermediate class decision is difficult, not only as to whether any operation is necessary, but as to the exact procedure required. It is in these cases especially that the more conservative line of treatment in the first instance has been found to promise the best results, and it is with these cases more particularly that the following remarks are concerned.

Nature of the injuries.

Apart from scalp wounds, the majority of gunshot wounds of the head are essentially compound fractures complicated by more or less serious injury to the brain and its membranes. The nature and extent of the damage to scalp and bone, and the presence or absence of a foreign body can be ascertained by inspection and X-ray examination, but the extent of the cerebral injury can be definitely determined only by evidence of disturbance of cerebral functions and a consideration of the factors that contribute to it.

Symptoms of injury to the brain.

Some of the symptoms of injury to the brain are only temporary, such as the effect of shock, local œdema or contusion, while others are due directly to the destruction of brain tissue, and vary according to the region injured.

It is apt to be too readily assumed that the symptoms which may exist at any given moment after receipt of the injury are related directly to some gross and visible lesion such as depressed bone. Such an assumption is likely to lead to the performance of an operation, having for its object the amelioration of the symptoms. In most cases such an operation is destined to failure, because the functional disturbance is rarely due to any pathological condition that can be directly affected by operation. The blow which has injured scalp and bone has also and at the same time injured the brain ; the lesions are co-existent but independent.

Infection.

Later another factor may come into play, namely, microbic infection. The importance of this factor is almost wholly dependent upon the integrity of the dura mater, and so vitally important is this membrane as a

Importance of the barrier afforded by the dura mater.

barrier against intracranial infection that it is rarely, if ever, justifiable to incise it in the presence of an open wound. In the majority of cases of gunshot wounds of the head the dura is already lacerated, but in spite of this, the subarachnoid space usually escapes direct infection owing to the rapid formation of adhesions between the dura and the pia-arachnoid round the opening. Any enlargement of the dural opening, therefore, in the course of an operation is liable to be followed by spread of infection, and should be resorted to only in exceptional conditions. Fortunately in most cases any intracerebral procedure which may be necessary for the removal of bone fragments, and for the drainage of the disintegrated and septic brain along their track, can be carried out quite well through the original opening in the dura without disturbance of these protective adhesions.

Before undertaking any operation it is desirable to have a clear idea as to what its aim is, what result is to be expected from it, and how best that result is likely to be attained. The operative objectives may be (1) The relief of symptoms of cerebral injury ; (2) The prevention of complications which might arise in future, and (3) The cleansing of the wound and removal of bone fragments and missiles. We may briefly examine each of these proposals. *Objects to be attained by operation.*

(1) **Relief of symptoms of cerebral injury.**—These symptoms may be general or local. The most prominent of the general symptoms are loss of consciousness, headache, slowing of the pulse rate, and (often quite early) blurring of the optic discs. Do these symptoms, which are due to a pathological increase of intracranial pressure, need immediate relief by operation ? The answer becomes clear when the underlying pathological basis is considered. Within the first two or three days the rise of pressure is due to traumatic œdema, usually associated with contusion, and small hæmorrhages in various situations both intracerebral and extracerebral. These lesions are not confined to the neighbourhood of the injury, for " contre- *Explanation of symptoms.*

coup" contusion is very common. The brain, in fact, is bruised and œdematous; the pressure so produced is rarely sufficiently high to require relief by operation. Occasionally a progressive hæmorrhage may cause an increasing rise of pressure, but this is very rarely met with in gunshot wounds, and when it does occur it gives rise to unmistakable signs, such as deepening coma, muscular flaccidity, slowing of the pulse rate, and stertorous breathing.

The prominent local symptoms commonly observed in these cases are paralysis, fits, alteration of reflexes, sensory disturbances, and visual defects; these are due either to destruction of cerebral tissue or to temporary functional disturbance by shock, contusion, local œdema and the like, which on the one hand cannot be influenced by operative interference, and on the other, tend to recover spontaneously. It is clear therefore that *operation is very rarely called for on account of cerebral symptoms whether general or local.*

Effects of retention of foreign bodies.

(2) **The prevention of symptoms which might develop later,** and especially of Jacksonian epilepsy, has occasionally been the direct object of an early operation, but as yet we know nothing of the probability of the occurrence of such later symptoms; and the risks which attend intracranial manipulations in the presence of a septic wound are such as to forbid the performance of an operation, whose sole object is the avoidance of some problematical future complication. The avoidance of abscess formation and septic encephalitis is more important, but comes under the next heading.

Nature of cranial operations.

(3) **The cleansing of the wound.**—Operations upon gunshot wounds of the head should be regarded primarily as cleansing operations. In general it may be said that the

sooner such procedures are undertaken the better ; but
certain conditions peculiar to this part of the body, as
well as certain considerations from the military stand-
point, render the universal application of this general rule
inadvisable or impracticable.

Although a certain amount of overlapping is unavoid-
able, it is possible to classify cranial injuries into certain
groups :—

(a) **Fissured fracture, or depressed fracture of the inner table without gross defect of bone.**—In the majority of these cases immediate trephining is not indicated. If the dura is uninjured, little or no harm might result from such an exploratory operation, though little good could be expected, but if the dura is torn in such a case, removal of the overlying bone is likely to be followed by intradural infection. In these cases, therefore, the treatment is that applicable to any dirty scalp wound. In slighter cases simple cleansing is all that is required ; in others it is best to excise the bruised and septic edges, leaving the result-ing wound open for drainage. If the aponeurosis is intact excision should not be done. Later, if X-ray examination were to reveal the presence of a gross depression, it might be advisable to operate if further symptoms develop. *[margin: Fractures without gross defect of bone.]*

(b) **Depressed fracture of the " gutter " type.**—In most of these cases the dura is injured, but unless brain is escaping or visible this cannot be determined with certainty. The probe should never be used to ascertain whether there is a hole in the dura. Where brain is not visible it is best to shave and cleanse the scalp and wound, and not to undertake a trephining operation immediately lest a hernia of the swollen brain should be started. The danger of waiting until the concussion stage has passed is less than that of operating before *[margin: Depressed fracture.]*

protective adhesions have formed between the dura and pia-arachnoid and shut off the subarachnoid space from infection.

The operation can be more safely undertaken after a few days, when a flap can be turned down so as to expose the whole area of injury, the damaged bone removed, and free drainage provided. If the dura be found intact it must on no account be interfered with. If, however, the dura be torn, any superficial in-driven fragments should be gently removed and drainage effected. In the absence of an X-ray examination no further search for bone fragments or missiles should be made.

Single wounds of the skull.

(c) **Single penetrating wounds of the cranial cavity.**— Immediate interference should take only the form of a cleansing operation. Without X-ray examination it is not possible to ascertain the presence, extent, or depth either of in-driven bone fragments or of pieces of metal; whilst at the same time, it is unsafe to undertake any intracerebral manipulation before the subarachnoid space is shut off by adhesions. As a rule, therefore, the immediate treatment should consist in widely shaving and disinfecting the scalp, excising the wound edges, washing away any protruding soft brain matter with a stream of hot saline, and applying an antiseptic dressing. The patient is then in a better condition to be sent to the base where a radiographic examination can be made, and further treatment carried out if necessary. Whenever time and opportunity permit, the whole head should be shaved, as what appear to be single penetrating wounds not infrequently turn out to be exit wounds, the small entrance wound elsewhere having been overlooked in a tangled mass of bloody hair.

Wounds traversing the skull.

(d) **Through-and-through wounds,** where the missile has traversed and emerged from the cranial cavity, are best treated by cleansing the entrance and exit wounds, and carefully watching for symptoms of compression which may follow the concussion stage. In most cases where the skull has been traversed by a bullet fired at close quarters the brain is so extensively injured by the explosive effect that the chance of survival is small.

(c) **Extensive comminuted fractures and large defects in the skull with considerable laceration of the brain,** such as frequently result from perforating wounds or from glancing blows by a large missile, are on the whole unfavourable, though many surprising recoveries have been observed from such injuries. As the wounds are invariably infected, the main aim of treatment should be the provision of efficient drainage. Adequate results can hardly be expected from extensive operations, and these on the one hand are rarely well borne, and on the other are liable to disseminate infection more widely and deeply without commensurate advantages. As a general rule these cases do not require operative treatment beyond dealing with the scalp wound, removing detached exposed fragments of bone and the exposed brain, according to the immediate indications. The protusion of much brain, or the development of a large hernia, may be subsequently controlled by a distant decompression or by repeated lumbar puncture.

Comminuted fractures.

Retained missiles.—It is not legitimate to search for a supposed retained missile in the absence of an X-ray examination, and a careful localization. The commonest variety found is a splinter of shell or shrapnel case; whole shrapnel bullets and rifle bullets are met with occasionally. The shell splinters are sometimes multiple; their removal, even when accurately localized is difficult and dangerous except when easily accessible. Many such

Retained missiles.

cases which have reached the base and been regarded as inoperable, have nevertheless gone home improved and improving. Attempts to remove easily accessible pieces may be made, but the risks of increased damage to the brain and of spreading infection must be considered. The use of the electro-magnet has enabled some of these cases to be dealt with more hopefully. Missiles which lie deeply in the cranial cavity, or have bounced back into the brain after impinging upon and sometimes fracturing the bone, should, as a rule, be left alone.

Importance of drainage. *The essential point in the treatment in every variety of wound must be the provision of adequate drainage of the damaged brain tissue.*

Closure of scalp wounds. **Closure of wounds in the scalp.**—In certain wounds which are not seriously infected, a more rapid and favourably recovery may be obtained by covering the exposed brain by scalp tissue, after it has been carefully cleansed by irrigation, and the disintegrated cerebral matter washed away; but efficient lateral drainage must be provided.

It is rarely possible to bring the edges of the excised scalp wound together, and even if this can be done, it makes the scalp flap so tense that proper drainage cannot be obtained from beneath it. A very satisfactory method of obtaining a covering is by dissecting flaps from the under surface of the scalp, which can be brought across and sutured to the under surface of the excised wound. Drainage is then obtained by a long well fenestrated tube which is placed across the dural opening and projects at each end from under the edges of the flap, or by two such tubes coming from opposite edges of the flap which meet at the dural opening. This permits free drainage and frequent irrigation of the cerebral wound.

Decompression.—Causes of increased intracranial pressure.

(1.) During the earliest stage the increase is due to contusion and œdema, and is rarely sufficiently severe to need operative relief.

(2.) Occasionally, but rarely, progressive hæmorrhage causes the rise of pressure. In such a case it may become necessary to open the dura freely and to evacuate the clot, but here the grave risk of infecting the subdural space should only be taken to save the patient from death by compression.

(3.) Later, increased pressure and development of a progressive hernia may be due to infection of the brain or its membranes, taking the form of meningitis, or spreading encephalitis. Local abscesses occasionally occur within two or three weeks of the injury; probably they will be found to be more frequent at a later date.

In view of the fact that the early rise of intracranial pressure is rarely of sufficient degree to require a decompressive operation, and that lumbar puncture will give at least temporary relief; that progressive hæmorrhage is in these cases a condition of great rarity; and that when widespread infection exists the majority of cases are hopeless (local abscesses excepted), it is clear that an operation of decompression is rarely called for. When such is required, however, it may be done locally or contralaterally.

The local operation introduces so great a risk of meningitis, as the dura has to be opened in the presence of a septic wound or around a septic hernia cerebri, that the advisability of performing a clean subtemporal decompression on the opposite side has to be considered. Good results have followed this operation on several occasions.

OPERATIVE TECHNIQUE.

A few points of which experience has proved the value, may be briefly mentioned :—

Irrigation.—Whenever possible the whole operation should be conducted under a constant stream of hot (115° F.) normal saline, or, if preferred, of a weak antiseptic solution (*e.g.*, 1-200 carbolic). This not only checks hæmorrhage and avoids the necessity of continued swabbing, but also washes away a quantity of infected material.

Excision of the scalp wound is usually advisable. It is not desirable to close the resulting gap by sutures, nor indeed is it possible to do so if the gap is of any considerable size. When the scalp wound has been excised and sutured, pus and gas may become pent up beneath a greatly œdematous scalp.

Incision.—The scalp incision should take the form of an omega flap sufficiently large to expose the bony lesion thoroughly, as well as a considerable area of skull around it. Linear incisions which traverse the wound or wounds, and crucial incisions are inadvisable, as they limit the field of operation. If the dura mater is opened, the edges of such a scalp incision, passing through the original wound are very liable to become septic and come into direct contact with the brain.

Removal of bone.—Less damage is done to the brain by working through a trephine hole made at a little distance from the fracture than by attempting to use the original opening as a starting point. An area of bone should be removed large enough to expose at least half an inch of normal dura around the wound in that membrane.

Treatment of exposed brain.—The greatest gentleness must be used so as not to disturb the adhesions which shut off the subarachnoid space. If bone fragments are indriven they must be removed, the finger gently feeling for them so as to direct the forceps by which removal is effected. Should the general pressure be so high as to render these manipulations difficult, owing to the bulging of brain into the opening, a lumbar puncture may be done. It is generally found that the removal of three or four drachms of fluid is sufficient to render manipulation of the brain easy.

Drainage of the track.—A piece of rubber tubing well fenestrated, as wide as can be conveniently introduced and rather shorter than the length of the track may be employed ; it can be kept in place by suturing it to the edges of the excised scalp wound. The disintegrated and necrotic tissue that forms the wall of the cavity is however liable to become compressed around the rubber tube and form a more or less impermeable wall between this and the softened and infected brain beyond, which latter is exactly the part that requires the most thorough drainage. It has been found that a perforated metal drainage tube answers the purpose better than rubber. Such a tube can easily be fashioned from the perforated zinc sheeting supplied as splinting material. The softened material in the wall of the track gradually escapes through the numerous holes into the interior of the tube, whence it can be removed by syringing with hydrogen peroxide. It has been found that pure sterile glycerine forms an admirable dressing for these cases ; the tube is filled with it and packed round with gauze soaked in glycerine. Good results have also been obtained by packing the tube with salt soloids, and by using a 5 per cent solution of salt in 1-200 carbolic. The tube should not be removed too soon ; it is usually kept in for eight to ten days.

Suture of the flap.—Although drainage of the space between flap and bone may be allowed for by leaving the original wound open, it is well to drain at the lateral angles of the flap also, for which purpose rolls of sheet rubber answer admirably.

Lumbar puncture is useful in relieving pressure either during the concussion stage or later. It is a safe procedure when the dura mater is intact, but considerable caution is necessary when this membrane is lacerated. In the latter circumstances the withdrawal of fluid may either cause a spread of infection directly, or the sudden reduction of pressure may, by allowing the brain to fall away from the surface, break down the adhesions between the pia-arachnoid and the dura mater, and so expose the meninges to infection.

When, therefore, lumbar puncture is done in the presence of a wounded dura mater, whether for diagnostic purposes or for the relief of pressure, only a small quantity of cerebro-spinal fluid, *e.g.* 2 to 6 drachms, should be removed at a time. The puncture may be, however, repeated frequently, if necessary.

Evacuation of men with head injuries.—Patients who are deeply insensible or even comatose must necessarily remain at the clearing station for several days at least, and in some cases operations must be performed before transmission to the base. When a case has been submitted to operation, the patient should be kept as quiet as possible for at least seven days before being moved.

Favourable cases should not be transferred from the base to England for at least two to three weeks after operation.

SPINAL INJURIES.

The spinal cord may be injured directly by the missile, or by in-driven fragments of the vertebral column which lacerate it or compress it, or indirectly by the concussion effect of a projectile, generally of high velocity, which touches the vertebral column. The latter condition, which is quite common, is found when the bullet has either passed through the body of the vertebra or touches the spinous, articular or especially the transverse process, and often occurs without any extensive fracture of the vertebræ.

The medullary changes produced vary ; in many cases, there are small scattered hæmorrhages, especially in the grey matter, occasionally a single large hæmorrhage, but more frequently œdematous swelling of the whole cord with considerable disintegration of its tissue and central softenings are found ; extensive extradural hæmorrhage is very rare.

The symptoms produced by these three types of injury are very similar and depend on the site and severity of the lesion. It is very difficult to determine the degree of the injury or the prospect of recovery in the earlier stages, as the loss of power is almost invariably complete at first ; and, as the knee-jerks are often absent for some days in even slight cases, this fact cannot be regarded as a sign of complete transverse lesion. The state of tone in the muscles of the lower limbs and the reflex movements that can be obtained from the soles are the only reliable indications.

Within the first two weeks stimulation of the soles generally gives no reflex response in the severest cases ; in less severe injuries there may be isolated flexion of the great toes, or this movement associated with contraction of the hamstrings, while in more favourable cases a withdrawal reflex of the limb with extension of the great toes, and often dorsiflexion of the foot (Babinski's sign) is obtained. Account must be taken of the level of the injury, as lesions of the lumbo-sacral cord and cauda equina more readily abolish these reflex movements and the tone of the muscles than more highly placed injuries. The early return of the knee and ankle jerks is a favourable sign.

Diagnosis from functional paraplegia.

As the symptoms of organic paraplegia may be easily confused with those of functional or hysterical paralysis, which is not infrequently observed, especially in men who have been buried in broken-in trenches or under sandbags, attention may be drawn to a few points in their differential diagnosis. In hysterical or functional paraplegia sphincter control is not affected, while retention of urine is invariably present in severe organic lesions. In the latter condition the limbs are always flaccid at first, while they are often rigid, or the tone of the muscles is increased, and the knee and ankle jerks are usually exaggerated, in hysterical palsy. Absence of these reflexes, on the other hand, is invariably evidence of organic injury. Babinski's sign, when present, is also, of course, evidence of organic disturbance. Further, in hysterical states there may be no sensory disturbance, or, if there be any loss, it may take the form of stocking or glove anæsthesia, or occupy a distribution not explicable by any single organic lesion.

Treatment of special injuries.

The Treatment of the spinal injuries of warfare is extremely disappointing. Operation is successful in only very rare cases, and should be undertaken only when X-ray examination shows a missile lying against the spinal cord, or when its passage has driven in fragments of bone on to the cord. Even in these cases the results of operative interference have not been promising. The danger of infection spreading to the meninges through a laceration in the dura mater, which had been closed by a piece of depressed bone or by a clot, must be considered. In the concussion cases, in which the cord is not injured directly by the missile or by fractured bone, operation can do but little good. There can be no doubt, however, that a certain proportion of the cases tend to recover and will regain useful power, but improvement must necessarily be very slow.

The main object of treatment must be the prevention of the complications which threaten life. Many cases of spinal injury die from associated wounds of the chest or abdomen, but the fatal termination in a large proportion of the others is due to cystitis and septic pyelonephritis. The greatest care is consequently necessary in the passage of the catheter, and urinary antiseptics should be administered to all patients from as early a stage as is practicable. Frequent irrigation of the bladder is equally important, both as a preventive measure and as a mode of treatment if infection has started. A solution of quinine sulphate, 1 to 2 grains to the ounce, has proved most satisfactory for this purpose. *Treatment of complications.*

Cases of paraplegia should be sent to the base hospital at once if possible, on account of the need for suitable beds and water cushions, and because they require special care in nursing. The bladder should always be emptied when the patient arrives at a clearing station and before he leaves it. *Transportation of cases of paraplegia.*

All serious cases should be transferred to England as soon as possible, but as the spinal injury may be aggravated in the course of transit, patients with slighter and recoverable lesions should be kept as quiet as possible at the base for two or three weeks. This especially holds good for those cases in whom the vertebral column is fractured, or when in-driven fragments compress the cord ; and more particularly for cases of concussion in the cervical region, in whom there is some evidence to show that secondary degenerative changes are liable to develop.

INJURIES TO THE PERIPHERAL NERVES.

Lesions of this nature are not dealt with in these memoranda, since their treatment may be more satisfactorily carried out on the arrival of patients in England. It need hardly be added that in the case of a large trunk divided and exposed in an open wound provisional measures to prevent retraction of the severed ends should be taken.

PENETRATING CHEST WOUNDS AS SEEN AT THE FRONT.

No doubt many men shot through the chest die in a few minutes, but of those who live long enough to reach a field ambulance or a clearing station the great majority recover. In these cases there is generally much shock, but in a few instances this is not the case. Breathing is usually very difficult and painful, and is associated with a great deal of spasm and severe choking, so that the patient feels that he is going to die for want of breath. Blood is very often, but not always, spat up, and in a minority of cases the hæmoptysis is severe. Even when little or no blood is expectorated, bleeding commonly occurs into the pleural cavity, and the usual symptoms of internal hæmorrhage are added to the dyspnoea. The pulse is consequently often very small and rapid (as much as 140), and the respiration 60 to 80 to the minute. The diaphragm is fixed, and the abdomen may be so hard as to suggest an injury to the peritoneum rather than to the lung. This may indeed be very deceptive. Extensive pneumothorax makes the dyspnoea much worse, but is not usually present.

The usual physical signs of lung injury are weakness of breath sounds, with or without râles, or, when the lung is collapsed, complete absence of a respiratory murmur; dullness on percussion if there is a hæmothorax; and there may be a loss of vocal vibrations. If there is much pneumothorax there is a boxy hyper-resonance, and usually considerable displacement of the heart. The bell-sound can also be elicited.

Surgical emphysema occurs in a minority of cases and is generally limited to the chest wall in the neigh-

Condition of cases seen at the front.

bourhood of the wound. It may, however, spread to the neck, face, and trunk, and cause great and general swelling; but it is never in any way dangerous to life, does not cause dyspnoea, and may consequently be neglected.

Primary treatment of chest wounds.

Treatment.—The most important treatment of all is absolute rest in the recumbent or semi-recumbent position, but the patient must to some extent be allowed to lie as he finds himself most comfortable. If symptoms are severe, no attempt should be made even to remove clothing, or to do more than place clean dressings over the wound. If the opening into the chest is large, so that air passes in and out during respiration, the skin around should be painted with iodine, and the opening of the wound firmly closed with antiseptic gauze covered in by strapping. A third of a grain of morphine should be given subcutaneously as soon as possible, so as to relieve the pain and spasm and allow of the other lung doing its work. The morphine should be repeated in smaller doses for the first day or two. Food must be limited to drinks, and these should be given frequently, but not in large quantities at a time, as it is undesirable to distend the stomach.

The patient is often much more comfortable after the first day or two has passed, but he may easily be made worse by movements, and these may also cause secondary haemorrhage. It is therefore most important that no move should be permitted for several days, but at the end of a week the patient should be sent to the base.

Date for removal of cases to base.

In all cases of wounded lung the temperature rises within the first day or two. It may rapidly mount to 102° F. or even 103°, and often remains above 100° for ten days or a fortnight, or even longer.

Hæmothorax.

This does not imply that there is an empyema, and is not to be taken as an indication for puncturing the pleural cavity. The presence of hæmothorax is rather to be taken as an indication for non-interference, for while the pleura is full of blood the collapsed lung usually ceases to bleed, and if the blood is withdrawn by tapping, and the lung expands, bleeding is almost certain to recur.

It is therefore to be accepted that tapping a hæmothorax is never to be practised in the early days after a wound of the lung. The same rule applies when dyspnœa is due to pneumothorax, for no real good can come from drawing off air which can rapidly accumulate again from the wounded lung, during the first week after the injury.

Another complication which occurs within the first day Bronchitis. or two in many cases is bronchitis, which affects both lungs. This may be very slight and of no importance ; but in some cases it is serious, for the secretion is usually very sticky and tenacious, being more or less mixed with blood, and the condition of the patient and of the thorax makes expulsion by coughing difficult and painful.

It has been found that great relief is usually obtained by the administration every three or four hours of a mixture containing three grains each of iodide of potassium and carbonate of ammonia, and the ordinary rules for treating bronchitis apply to these patients also.

The unwounded lung is sometimes affected by pneumonia and pleurisy.

PENETRATING CHEST WOUNDS AT THE BASE HOSPITALS.

Hæmoptysis occurs sooner or later in nearly all Hæmorr- wounds that perforate the lung or drive broken ribs into hage.

its substance. Its occurrence is therefore always regarded
as a symptom indicating injury of the lung. But a gunshot wound of the chest wall alone, where the parietal
pleura is intact, may be accompanied by hæmoptysis, the
blood then being derived from the infarction and bruising
of the underlying lung, which is not directly wounded.

There is often free bleeding into the pleural cavity.
The blood may be derived from injured vessels in the
chest wall, but it has been proved, post-mortem, that in
the majority of cases it is derived from the lung vessels,
so that it is safer in deciding on the treatment suitable in
any given case to act on the assumption that the blood has
leaked from them. The bleeding usually ceases early, at
some time before the fourth or fifth day. Evidence of later
intrapleural hæmorrhage has been noted, but it is rare.

Effects of
intra-
thoracic
bleeding on
the lung.
As the blood accumulates within the cavity of the
chest, it compresses the lower lobes of the lung and
drives the air out of their alveoli. In consequence of this
the breath sounds over the collapsed lung in the lower
part of the chest are often tubular in character and may
give rise on physical examination to a mistaken diagnosis
of pneumonia. The lung at a higher level is over-
distended and emphysematous. In the largest effusions
the whole lung is collapsed against the mediastinum.

Coagulation
of the
effused
blood.
Clotting of the effused blood within the chest takes
place probably in all cases, and usually within the first
four or five days. But the character of the clotting is
unlike that which occurs in blood outside the body, and
it is still imperfectly understood. The chief difference
lies in the fact that the red cells as a rule do not remain
completely entangled in the clot. Hence the commonest
type of fluid withdrawn from a hæmothorax is very like
that of a simple, dark red, non-clotted blood. On standing, however, it does not clot fully, but yields a yellowish

red serum above a heavy deposit of free red cells. In the serum a fine gelatinous clot may form, and this is presumably a secondary phenomenon.

The form of the primary clot varies, and the following types have been noted :— Forms of primary clot.

1. That laid down in dense fibrinous laminae on the lung and parietal pleura, from which there is an early and complete separation of a yellowish red serum, in which free red cells remain floating in amounts that vary so much that the fluid may be either yellowish red, brownish red, or deep red and opaque like ordinary blood. Laminated.

2. A finely shredded clot, which passes easily through the needle and falls down in a precipitate with the red blood corpuscles when the fluid is allowed to stand. Shredded.

3. A massive and persistent clot, which occupies the pleural cavity like a jelly and yields very little fluid on aspiration. Massive.

4. A uniformly viscous fluid that is very difficult to withdraw through a needle. Viscous fluid.

In addition to the general symptoms of fever caused by absorption from the effused blood, there is a mild inflammation of the pleural membranes which results in a preliminary exudate of polymorphonuclear cells ; but in sterile cases this soon subsides, giving place to a fluid in which pleural endothelial cells and small mononuclear lymphocytes predominate. It is during this period that there are introduced into the serum substances which have the power to form a secondary soft gelatinous clot when the serum is withdrawn from the chest. Hence a sterile fluid from a hæmothorax in the second or third week after primary clotting may be very like that of a simple pleural effusion, and may be almost entirely free from the red cells which were entangled in the primary clot. It gives a secondary light gelatinous clot ; and its colour is yellowish or reddish brown. Nature of the secondary exudation.

Cellular emphysema and pneumothorax.

Air, as well as blood, often enters the pleural cavity from the injured lung or chest wall. From this it may be driven out by coughing and produce surgical emphysema around the wound; or it may accumulate within in such an amount as to cause an obvious pneumo-hæmothorax or even a complete pneumothorax. Relatively, these cases are not very common. Small intrapleural collections of air are frequent, but they are of no special importance from the point of view of treatment, and are mainly of interest owing to the clinical problem of distinguishing such cases from those of simple hæmothorax.

Nature of wound track in the lung.

As a rule the track of the missile through the lung is not a simple penetrating wound, but is accompanied by infarction and laceration to a varying degree. Extensive laceration is rare.

Causes of death.

Death may be caused in two ways; either as a direct result of the wound from hæmorrhage or pneumothorax; or indirectly by infection. Pure hæmorrhage is fatal only in the first few days, that is, it is the cause of death, in the men who succumb on the field or in the stations near the front. A few have died in the general hospitals at the base as the result of a simple hæmothorax, but never later than the first week after the wound.

It has been repeatedly found by autopsies on those who have died with progressive dyspnœa and cyanosis from the fourth or fifth day onwards that the fatality was not the result, as is generally supposed, of continued bleeding, but that it was due to the rapid development of an infection in the hæmothorax.

Death from hæmoptysis is practically unknown in the base hospitals. Primary hæmorrhage at the front, infection, but not secondary hæmorrhage, at the base, are the two principal causes of death.

Infection is unfortunately common, and unless promptly recognized, it is very disabling to the patient and frequently fatal. It occurs in perhaps 1 out of 4 of the large effusions, and it is introduced at the time of the actual wound. Bacteriological examination has proved that the infections of a hæmothorax fall into three main groups; those by streptococci and staphylococci; those by anaerobic bacilli; and those by the influenza bacillus, pneumococcus, and other organisms commonly found in the respiratory tract. The last group is derived from the injured lung, and infection from this source certainly does not occur in more than one out of five infected cases. Most of the infection is sown from without, comprising the first two groups of the skin cocci, and of the anaerobic bacilli of fæcal or soil contamination. *Frequency of infection*

Nature of the infection.

Jagged fragments of shell casing are especially dangerous, because they are more likely than rifle or shrapnel bullets to carry in shreds or pieces of clothing together with associated infectious material. *Danger of shell fragments.*

The organisms that are introduced may at once multiply freely in the effused blood before it clots, or they may be shut off within a mass of blood-clot and only later penetrate the free fluid. Their poisons often hæmolyse the blood corpuscles and so may give to the serum a characteristic carmine-red tint. Inflammation of the pleural membranes soon follows, with tenderness in the side, and the outpouring of innumerable pus cells. The later accumulation of these dying cells changes the fluid from a translucent red serum to a turbid one, brown in colour, or even frankly purulent and often offensive in odour. *Results of infection.*

As the infection increases, it may spread to the other side of the chest and excite a coarse, dry pleurisy, or more rarely an effusion and empyema; or it may remain *Spread to opposite side of chest.*

localized and lead to a great thickening of the visceral and parietal pleura that hinders subsequent re-expansion of the lung. Infective pericarditis is not common. It should be noted in reservation that a contralateral dry pleurisy may occur as a complication in a presumably sterile hæmothorax, and that blood in the pericardium produces the sound of pericardial friction.

Importance of early recognition of infection. These infections are often fatal, and the chief clinical problem in dealing with wounds of the chest is the early recognition of sepsis, so that it may be properly and promptly dealt with. Failure to realise this may cost a soldier his life, or at the least submit him to a wasting fever of unnecessary length, from which convalescence is very slow.

The clinical features of the various forms of chest wounds are as follows:—

Clinical features of hæmothorax. **Simple Hæmothorax.**—The patient has considerable dyspnœa which quietens down in a few days. Except for this and feverish restlessness at night, he feels fairly well. The temperature may rise to 103° F. with a regular daily oscillation, and the rise last for a fortnight with a smooth curve of decline. The tongue remains clean, and the pulse is rarely more than 100. There may be a slight icteric tinge of the conjunctivæ. In the second week the patient generally begins to recover strength and a healthy colour returns to his cheeks.

The affected side moves poorly with respiration, and the heart is displaced. The percussion note is dull over the fluid, hyper-resonant over the emphysematous lung that floats above it. Tactile fremitus is characteristically lost. The breath sounds are weak or distantly tubular over the fluid, while they are harsh over the hyper-resonant (Skodaic) area above. The vocal resonance is diminished, or increased with ægophony, in accordance with the state of the compressed lung beneath. There are no adventitious sounds, except the extraneous ones due to the frequent complication of subcutaneous surgical emphysema. The latter condition, of course, introduces a superficial tympanitic note on percussion, which entirely hides the true state beneath. Such a picture of fever, dyspnœa, dulness, and tubular breathing sometimes leads to a mistaken diagnosis of pneumonia.

Pneumonia may be recognised by the more markedly tubular character of its breath sounds, and especially by the presence of râles, and the absence of cardiac displacement. The condition sometimes appears on the side opposite to a hæmothorax, but a lung collapsed by the pressure of effused blood seems to be especially resistant to inflammatory changes, so that a hæmothorax and pneumonia practically never occur together on the same side. *Care needed in not confusing signs with those of pneumonia. Contra lateral pneumonia.*

Bronchitis is often aggravated by the injury, and the development of this disease in its purulent form is an especially fatal complication. *Bronchitis.*

Treatment at the front.—To avoid pneumonia or bronchitis, the wounded man should as soon as possible be well covered up. As far as is practicable, he must be spared all unnecessary movement, and morphia is needed to ensure rest and check coughing. Strapping the chest is of little value, because the wounded side soon assumes an immobility of its own. *Treatment of hæmothorax.*

If blood leaks from the wound, and air is sucked in and out through it, infection will quickly extend from the skin. This must be controlled. If the leak cannot be checked by a dressing applied to the surface, the hole should be superficially plugged with clean gauze soaked in some antiseptic, such as weak carbolic lotion.

Transference to the base.

At the end of a week at the latest the patient should, as a rule, be moved on to the base hospitals. There is then little risk of further hæmorrhage, whereas there is great danger in delaying surgical treatment of an infected hæmothorax. Infection generally requires bacteriological proof of its presence before a rib is resected, and in some cases it is only at the base that facilities for this can be satisfactorily obtained. The most dangerous of all are the fulminating forms of infection by gas-producing bacilli. These infections are sometimes wrongly viewed as being merely an aggravation of a simple pneumo-hæmothorax. If the error is not corrected and the chest soon opened, the patient dies.

Treatment at the base.

At the base hospitals.—Small effusions, that do not reach more than a couple of inches above the angle of the scapula and do not cause much displacement of the heart, may be left alone for cure by natural absorption. Larger ones should be aspirated, because absorption is slow when the pleural surface has been coated with blood-clot, and the lung in consequence will expand imperfectly. Further, the duration of the pyrexia is considerably shortened by aspiration.

Aspiration.

With ordinary care for asepsis, a sterile hæmothorax can be aspirated without any risk of infection. Those in which an empyema has developed after aspiration are almost always cases that were infected from the outset, though this was not obvious because the infected blood does not assume a purulent appearance until some time has elapsed. The aspiration should not be attempted earlier than the sixth or seventh day, and in general it should be delayed until fresh hæmoptysis has ceased. At any time evacuation is liable to be incomplete in consequence of clotting of the blood within the chest and imperfect separation of the serum.

It is impossible to lay down any satisfactory rule as to the best time for aspiration, because the time at which clotting takes place and the extent to which the serum separates from the clot vary so widely in different cases. There are, moreover, no physical signs known which will serve to indicate whether the chest contains fluid or clotted blood. Pain and coughing during the operation might dislodge clot from the lung and cause fresh hæmorrhage, though such an accident has not once been seen in a large series of aspirations. To avoid it the skin and particularly the parietal pleura should be anæsthetized with 2 per cent novocaine. The skin should be pierced with a scalpel and a trochar and blunt-nosed canula should be used. The sharp-pointed aspirating needle is dangerous to the underlying lung, and should not be employed. A curious feature of these cases is that the diaphragm is often immobile as well as the chest wall, and that it tends to rise up high inside the chest. This abnormal position of the diaphragm must be borne in mind when the trochar is being introduced, and still more so in cases where resection of a rib is made necessary by the presence of infection. As the fluid is removed, the lung expands, and the patient feels short of breath and inclined to cough. A preliminary injection of morphia will lessen this reaction. It can be entirely controlled by using apparatus (*e.g.*, Parry Morgan's) to replace the blood by intrapleural injection of oxygen, which is then slowly absorbed in the next few days. Otherwise the aspiration must be carried out slowly, or completed on a later day. Aspiration with oxygen replacement not only prevents any unpleasant or dangerous symptoms, but also enables much more of the effused blood to be withdrawn, and the operation is then free from all discomfort.

Where clotting has taken place in mass and the serum is imperfectly separated, it will be found that the fluid runs out by fits and starts from the needle, and that the patient soon feels tightness in the chest, though only a small amount has been withdrawn where it was anticipated from the physical signs that two or three pints would be obtained. In these circumstances it is useless to make any further trial until several weeks have elapsed.

The clot tends to lie chiefly at the back of the pleural cavity, so that the aspiration is most likely to succeed when the trochar is introduced well forward in the axilla near the anterior limit of the area of dulness.

Bacteriological examination of product of aspiration. Wherever facilities exist, a sample of the fluid withdrawn should be examined bacteriologically for a primary infection. This is readily taken by the syringe that is used for the local anæsthetic. The characters of an infected fluid are given below. A sterile fluid from clotted blood yields a white or brownish froth, never carmine coloured ; it is itself of a reddish brown transparent tint.

When a sterile haemothorax has been completely aspirated, the fluid does not reaccumulate.

Transference of patients with wound of the lung. It is important that men with wounds of the lung should not be sent across the sea earlier than a fortnight after the injury. Three weeks is a safer time-limit to guard against the risk of a fresh hæmorrhage or pneumothorax.

Pneumo-hæmothorax physical signs. **Pneumo-hæmothorax.**—The dyspnœa is greater and the displacement of the heart more extreme. Over the resonant area breath sounds are very weak, and tactile fremitus is diminished, but the vocal resonance is often almost normal. This weakness of breath sounds of a pneumothorax is often mimicked in a chest where there is only emphysematous lung above a hæmothorax, and where the increased intrapleural pressure and comparative immobility of the injured side of the chest combine to check the current of air that should pass up and down the bronchial ramifications. A bell-sound may or may not be obtained. The most useful sign is the change of level of the line of fluid dulness as the patient is raised from the horizontal to a sitting posture. X-rays reveal a characteristic horizontal level of the fluid, which also moves with change of posture.

These cases are not peculiarly liable to infection, because infection from the respiratory tract is relatively uncommon. But inasmuch as infection in them would be especially disabling with a lung so fully collapsed, they should be aspirated. If possible, aspiration should be delayed until about the twelfth day so that the air-leak from the lung may be sealed. The fluid should be removed first by dipping the canula, and then withdrawing the air, provided that its removal does not cause marked distress and dyspnœa in the patient. *Rarity of infection from the respiratory tract.*

Pneumothorax.—This occurs occasionally with a minimal effusion of blood. The heart is greatly displaced and the breath sounds are practically abolished. The percussion note is resonant, and the vocal resonance has a peculiar chinking reverberation. The bell-sound with two coins is generally obtained with ease. *Signs of pneumothorax.*

The dyspnœa soon quietens down. After a fortnight or more the air should be withdrawn slowly by aspiration so as to aid the expansion of the lungs.

Infected Haemothorax.—Infection always develops when the wound has remained open and leaked blood for some time. In closed wounds it is especially frequent where the X-rays reveal an embedded fragment of shell. Fracture of the ribs does not predispose to it, except where the wound over them is open.

Signs of the occurrence of infection in a haemothorax.
The wounded man soon looks ill, and, his appearance daily becomes worse. The tongue is furred, and either white and tremulous, or brown and dried. The temperature oscillates widely. Very characteristic is the increase of the pulse rate, to 120 or beyond, though even in severe infections it may be no more than 90. Soon pain and tenderness are complained of in the infected side, as the pleural inflammation develops. But it must be remembered that subcutaneous surgical emphysema itself often causes tenderness. In the acute cases the dyspnœa increases with distressing rapidity.

Contralateral pleurisy.
A pleurisy, coarse or fine, often appears on the opposite side, especially in the streptococcal cases. Infection by anaerobic gas-forming bacilli may lead to a very rapid
Anaerobic infections.
development of symptoms, with a flushed face, high fever, suddenly increased displacement of the heart, and the appearance of a *cracked pot percussion note* over the localized area in the chest where the gas is forming. Hæmolytic jaundice may also develop after a few days.

Neglect of such cases is fatal, whereas life can generally be saved by early drainage at the beginning of, or during, the second week.

Where infection is suspected, the chest must be explored and the fluid examined bacteriologically. If infection is found and the effusion is very large, it may be best to aspirate first and resect a rib some days later, so
Resection of ribs.
that the lung may partly expand before resection and perhaps develop adhesions which will lessen the size of the subsequent empyema cavity. Otherwise immediate resection is best, the lowest rib possible, either the 9th or 10th being chosen, bearing in mind the tendency of the diaphragm to rise, and a couple of inches excised. A local anæsthetic should be employed for the operation, where the lungs are seriously affected.

Cases which are leaking blood or pus from a wound high up in the chest almost invariably require another opening by resection at the lowest point at which drainage is practicable.

It is dangerous to dislodge much of the infected blood clot at the time of the resection, since this may break down inflammatory barriers and allow the infecting organisms to develop a septicæmia. Subsequent irrigation of the empyema cavity with weak hydrogen peroxide together with some antiseptic lotion will help to remove the infected clots. The latter, as they come away later, are sometimes mistaken for sloughs of the lung. It is important that means should be used for their removal, since their retention within the cavity prolongs the fever in much the same way as septic fragments of placenta in the uterus are found to do. *Caution with regard to removal of clot.*

So far as the ultimate history of these cases has been traced yet, it is found that the lungs slowly re-expand, and the sinus is closed in from two to four months without the need for any further operation.

The criteria of infection in the sample of infected blood are as follow :—

1.—A very offensive smell, like that of rotten eggs, caused by anaerobic bacilli. This in itself at once justifies and necessitates resection, but this test will obviously not be relied upon, if the means for a bacteriological examination are at hand. *Criteria of infection.*

2.—A crimson fluid with a froth that remains of a deep carmine red throughout aspiration, due to hæmolysis by an organism.

3.—A brownish red turbidity and opaqueness—caused by the pouring out of pus cells. This should be confirmed by letting the fluid stand for an hour or more, preferably with the addition of an equal volume of 3 per cent.

potassium citrate solution to prevent secondary clotting. Any deposit of white or brownish pus at the bottom of the test tube is then sufficient justification for resection.

4.—The recognition of organisms by microscopic methods in a film stained with methylene blue or otherwise. Cultures occasionally give evidence of infection where immediate films have failed.

Test No. 2 should raise suspicion of infection, but it is insufficient evidence unless confirmed by No. 4, and the recognition of organisms by direct microscopic and cultural methods should always be resorted to where it is practicable. The secondary clot hinders the preparation of microscopic films, and it is therefore a great help if the sample that is to be examined in this way is at once mixed with an equal volume of 3 per cent potassium citrate solution. The latter can be conveniently kept in sterilized vaccine tubes. A moderate number of polymorphs in a microscopic film does not justify resection, because these may be the result of a sterile inflammatory reaction. But a deposit of pus visible to the naked eve in a tube is enough, even though the organism cannot be recognized.

Rarity of spontaneous recovery after repeated aspirations.

The cases in which a bacterial infection or a serious purulent infection have ultimately vanished without other treatment than that of repeated aspirations are so few that it is probably unwise to submit the patient to the risk of being left with a closed infection of the chest.

Lacerated Wounds of the Lung.—These are seen where there is extensive fracture of the ribs ; and when the outer wound is only partly closed they are the most fatal of all. Sometimes there is no hæmothorax, and death then may come speedily with a spreading septic pneumonia. Against such a pulmonary infection the existence of a hæmothorax is an actual safeguard, even though the effused blood itself be infected.

Wounds in which the chest wall has been widely torn open frequently recover well. Hence it seems probable that enlargement of the partly-closed wounds, in which there is no hæmothorax, so as to provide for free drainage, might be attempted. But the operation is dangerous, and it is not always advisable.

RETAINED FOREIGN BODIES IN THE CHEST.

Rifle bullets and most shrapnel balls lodged within the chest cavity or in the lungs should not be removed. This rule may be relaxed if the bullets lie loose within the pleura and on the diaphragm, and give rise to pain or discomfort. Treatment of retained bullets.

Pieces of shell or shrapnel case should be removed from the mediastina if practicable, but if they are lodged in the lung they should usually only be dealt with as a secondary measure. Shell and shrapnel case.

WOUNDS OF THE ABDOMEN AS SEEN AT THE FRONT.

Immediate condition of the patient.

The condition of patients suffering from these injuries as seen at the front varies very widely in proportion to the part involved and the viscera injured, but in very general terms it may be stated that the two chief complications of all abdominal wounds are (1) hæmorrhage and (2) perforation of the hollow viscera.

Apart, therefore, from the shock due to the extensive visceral lesions, the first danger to the patient is the hæmorrhage, and there can be no doubt that this is a much more frequent cause of death than is peritonitis.

A large number of men shot through the abdomen die on the field, and many more survive for only a short time after their arrival at a field ambulance. The remainder present at first the ordinary symptoms of shock and loss of blood. They are commonly blanched and have a small and rapid pulse. Pain is generally severe, but in some cases is not very marked, and if the wound is in the

Simulation of thoracic injury.

upper part of the abdomen the chief difficulty may be in breathing, so that the condition may simulate that of injury to the lungs. The abdomen is hard, and at first retracted, but after an interval of some hours it is often flatulent. It usually does not move well on respiration, but both the hardness and the fixation may be limited to that part of the abdomen which has been wounded, and even if no hollow viscus has been perforated, an abdomen which is full of blood may be very hard and fixed, and vomiting may be quite as severe as when the intestine is injured. The majority of the patients who arrive at a clearing station are too ill to permit of any operation being done, but in some an exploration must be taken into consideration.

Wounds in the area occupied by the small intestine are certainly more fatal than those of the flanks or upper part of the abdomen, and patients with injuries to the solid viscera, such as the liver and the kidneys, recover from bullet wounds in the majority of cases. Wounds caused by shell fragments, and especially large fragments, are commonly fatal whatever region is injured. It must also be remembered that very many bullets which enter the buttocks or flanks pass forward into the abdomen, and, on account of the thickness of tissue through which they pass, a considerable number of the missiles are retained. It is well therefore to be always suspicious as to the presence of internal injury in a case of wound of the lumbar or gluteal regions, and not only must the intestines be kept in mind, but the bladder also is very liable to be hit in these cases.

WOUNDS OF THE DIFFERENT VISCERA.

The Liver.—Most patients with bullet wounds of the liver passing from front to back, or vice versa, who arrive at clearing stations, recover. No doubt many others die earlier from hæmorrhage, and some also die in the clearing stations from the same cause. A few of those who survive develop peritonitis, without gross suppuration, owing to the escape of bile, and in some of these jaundice is very marked.

The Kidney is often injured without any dangerous symptoms arising. Haematuria is not usually severe, but it may be both severe and continuous. In some cases the bleeding ceases for a time only to return later, and in these cases the kidney is often found much lacerated.

The Stomach.—Many bullets appear to pass through the stomach without causing severe symptoms, but much, of course, depends on whether or not it is distended with food.

If it is distended with food, the symptoms of perforation are likely to be present, but if not, and if care is observed in feeding, no bad effects necessarily ensue. A large proportion of patients with wounds in the stomach region survive.

The Large Intestine.—Wounds in the flanks, in the area of the colon, often show at first no evidence of perforation of the bowel. In others fæcal matter escapes at once, or, more commonly, it begins to discharge in two or three days. Either peritonitis or cellulitis may develop and lead to a fatal issue.

The Small Intestine.—It appears probable that most wounds of the small intestines are fatal. There is no doubt that some patients shot directly through the "small intestine area" do recover, but it does not necessarily follow that in all cases the intestine is wounded. It must be clearly kept in mind in all abdominal wounds, and especially in those of the intestines, that when a bullet traverses the abdominal cavity the injuries it inflicts are commonly multiple. Not only are several coils of small bowel usually shot through, but the same bullet may wound also the large bowel or extensively lacerate the mesentery or the vessels of the omentum, and may injure also the solid viscera. It necessarily follows that such patients bleed from many injured places, and it may be said truly that if a man with a wounded intestine dies within 36 hours his death is due to bleeding and not to the fact that a hollow viscus was perforated. In the majority of cases of wounds of the small intestine there is practically no escape of the contents.

Multiple
nature of
the injuries.

In those cases where the bullet has passed more superficially and has only just entered the peritoneal cavity the injury is often less extensive, and not so many coils of intestine are involved.

In many instances when the patient has survived for several days, a post-mortem examination has shown that the bowel above the lesion is greatly distended with gas and fluid which had not escaped through the wounded coil. Whatever theory may be suggested to account for this, the practical fact is that these patients die as much from atonic obstruction as from peritonitis, and operations have shown exactly similar conditions to those found at autopsies. *Condition of the bowel as revealed at post-mortem examination.*

In those patients who survive the loss of blood, but do badly, the ordinary signs of peritonitis and atonic obstruction quickly develop. The abdomen becomes distended with flatus, hard and tender, pain is severe, the pulse quick and feeble, and the tongue dry and furred. Vomiting is usual, and may become fæculent, but in not a few cases it is absent or slight. Some patients who do well for the first three or four days then get worse and die, and it is difficult to say when a man is safe with a wound which from its symptoms seems to have injured the gut. *Clinical course of intestinal wounds.*

TREATMENT OF ABDOMINAL WOUNDS.

The performance of primary operations on patients suffering from abdominal wounds is only rarely indicated. *General treatment of intestinal wounds.*

In some patients the state of collapse is so extreme that operation is evidently out of the question, while in others it is clear that no one incision could possibly expose the whole of the organs which lie in the track of the missile. An exploration frequently fails to disclose all the points

(11379)   H from which bleeding has originated, while even at a post-mortem examination the position of a retained missile may be difficult to discover.

In considering an operation the conditions and surroundings of the patient before and after its performance must also be given due weight.

If no operation is thought advisable, the patient should be kept at absolute rest in the semi-recumbent position, and small doses of morphia should be given. Pituitary extract is often useful in combating collapse and in preventing flatulent distension. If shock is present, half a pint to a pint of normal saline with 5 per cent glucose together with a tablespoonful of brandy may be given per rectum, or saline solution may be given either subcutaneously or intravenously.

Administration of nourishment. If solid viscera only are injured, fluid nourishment may be given in fair quantities, and this holds good also in cases of injury to the lower segments of the colon. Even if the small intestine or cæcum is wounded, no harm can follow the swallowing of a tablespoonful of hot water every hour or oftener ; this makes the patient more comfortable and less restless, while if he is suffering from loss of blood and lack of fluid in the tissues the advantage is obvious. In patients who can take no nourishment by mouth, the rectal infusions of saline with glucose may be continued, due consideration being given to the height of the injury in the intestine.

After the first four or five days an attempt to get rid of flatus may be made by giving a subcutaneous injection of pituitary extract, and twenty minutes later introducing a couple of ounces of glycerine into the rectum. Aperients should not at first be given by the mouth if the stomach or intestine have been wounded.

INDICATIONS FOR OPERATION.

Wounds of the **Liver**, passing through its whole thickness in any diameter, should not be operated upon, for most of them do well, and it is usually impossible to deal with an injury of its posterior surface. But wounds of the surface of the liver due to the superficial passage of bullets across it from side to side may be advantageously operated upon *if there are symptoms indicating continued bleeding.* It is sometimes possible to arrest this by deep sutures of catgut or by gauze packing. Wounds of the liver.

If the **Gall Bladder** is wounded and the lesion can be diagnosed, drainage, as in cholecystostomy, is the best treatment. Wounds of the gall bladder.

Wounds of the **Kidney** should not be operated upon unless continued bleeding endangers life ; it is seldom that any operation short of nephrectomy can be done. Wounds of the kidney.

Wounds of the **Spleen** alone must be very rare, and no operation should be undertaken merely because the wound is in the splenic region. It may be advisable to operate when symptoms of continued bleeding are associated with such an injury. Wounds of the spleen.

Small Intestine.—In considering this question the first thing to note is that out of a good many operations for suture or resection of the gut there have as yet been few recoveries. In the next place, it must be recalled that in very few cases is there a single uncomplicated perforation. These facts taken into consideration with the condition of the patient and his surroundings make it quite clear that operations for wounds of the small intestine area are not to be done as a rule. Then it must also be constantly kept in mind that a positive diagnosis Results of operations for wounds of the small intestine.

is very difficult in many cases, and that in not a few wounds which appear to have perforated the gut there is really no such injury.

Patients to be sent to clearing stations as soon as possible. The next point to realise is, that to obtain the best results from operation, all men with abdominal wounds should be sent to clearing stations as expeditiously as possible, and this should be done in every case unless the patient is already too ill to admit of his being moved, for operations of this class should not be done in the field ambulances ; and unless all abdominal cases are sent on without delay, it will often be found impossible to move a patient on whom an operation becomes advisable.

It is evident that if several days have passed, and peritonitis is advanced, operations can seldom be of use.

Indications for operation. Under the following conditions a primary operation may reasonably be performed :—

(*a*) If a patient is seen within twelve to twenty-four hours of his injury, and if his general condition is good. (*b*) If the wounds of entry and exit are near together so as to indicate that only a small part of the whole abdomen has been traversed. (*c*) If by the protrusion of omentum or other evidence obtained on examination it is certain that the peritoneum is already opened. (*d*) If the patient is observed to have become worse than a few hours previously. (*e*) If the conditions for doing an operation are satisfactory. (*f*) If a rise in the pulse rate or increasing rigidity of the abdomen occur at a slightly later date, provided the patient is in good condition.

Treatment of perforations. If perforated bowel is found at the operation, it must not be assumed that other perforations do not exist, for such are usually present. It must also be realized that extensive injury to the mesentery is just as bad as laceration of the gut. In consequence of these conditions mere suture of a wound can very seldom be performed, and resection of the intestine is nearly always required, while, in not a few cases, operations reveal injuries so extensive that they cannot be repaired.

On the other hand, it must be remembered that it is only by a complete examination of the whole length of the intestine that its real condition can be ascertained, and if a search reveals that there are no perforations at all, it is evident that such a prolonged examination in a man depleted by bleeding may be sufficient to turn the balance against the chance of recovery.

In several cases perforated intestine has been found already protruding through the abdominal wound, and in some of these the gut has been sutured *in situ* to the abdominal wall and left to drain. This method of treatment may also be adopted in cases where suture or resection cannot be completed, but very few such cases can survive.

In all operations for gunshot wounds of the intestine recurrent bleeding is very liable to cause death, even if resection is satisfactorily performed. This is due to the fact that the blood already in the peritoneum makes it very difficult to discern all bleeding points in the omentum, mesentery, and subperitoneal tissues, and these should always be very carefully examined before the operation is finished. Recurrence of hæmorrhage.

Wounds of the Colon.—If there is an opening insufficient to permit of the free passage of fæces it should be enlarged, but where the sigmoid flexure or the descending colon is involved, and the bowel is found to be much torn, it is better to do a colostomy.

Wounds of the Rectum.—If these involve the peritoneum, colostomy may be done, but the prospects of recovery are very small.

Wounds of the Bladder.—The wound may involve the peritoneum, and in that case is almost always complicated by injuries to the intestines, so that there is little expectation of recovery. Where the wound is extra-peritoneal the rectum is also often opened. Whether this is so or not, the man is usually unable to micturate, and if a catheter is passed, the urine is found to be bloodstained. In other cases extravasation occurs, and the tenderness and swelling in the supra-pubic region may simulate peritonitis.

Retained missiles in the bladder. In several cases the missile has lodged in the bladder and given rise to very severe pain and frequent attempts to pass water. When this is the case, or when there is extravasation, the proper treatment is to explore the bladder above the pubes, and this is much facilitated by passing a silver catheter so as to push up the bladder well into the wound.

Wounds of the Urethra and Prostatic Region.—In some cases urination is not prevented, in others a catheter can be passed. If urine is retained and cannot be evacuated, either the urethra in the perineum must be opened, or else a supra-pubic cystotomy must be done.

TREATMENT OF WOUNDS OF THE ABDOMEN AT THE BASE HOSPITALS.

Wounds of the abdomen commonly arrive at the base hospitals several days after the injury. At this period it is rare that any operation can be undertaken, except as a secondary measure to relieve complications. It must be borne in mind that a considerable proportion of injuries, apparently thoracic, or of wounds of the buttock or thigh, may eventually prove to be complicated by abdominal or pelvic visceral injury. This is especially the case where the projectile is retained, and for this reason all patients with such injuries should be subjected to an early X-ray examination.

Where wounds of the intestinal tract are suspected or known to have occurred, great care should be exercised in the commencement of feeding. In early cases rectal saline infusions containing glucose may be given, and later fluid nourishment commenced with caution. No attempt should be made to obtain an action of the bowels before the end of seven days from the date of receipt of injury, and where the large intestine or the pelvic portion of the small intestine is the seat of injury, it should be borne in mind that the mechanical disturbance resulting from the administration of a large enema is more dangerous than a purgative given by the mouth. An injection of 1 oz. of glycerine is free from this objection, provided that the rectum is not the seat of injury. *(Wounds of the alimentary tract.)*

When an oral purgative is required small repeated doses of calomel ½ gr. every four hours, followed by a saline purgative, are recommended, or castor oil may be given.

Prolapse of Omentum is not uncommon. The tag of omentum should be ligatured at its base and removed. At the time of arrival at a base hospital, the omentum is already firmly adherent to the wound track, while replacement is obviously dangerous. It should be remembered that prolapse of uninjured omentum may be accompanied by serious internal injuries more or less distant within the abdomen. *(Treatment of prolapsed omentum.)*

Intraperitoneal Hæmorrhage.—Collections of blood may become infected and need to be evacuated. The signs are usually those of a localized intraperitoneal abscess, often tympanitic from the presence of gas.

Retroperitoneal Hæmorrhage.—Here again secondary infection may lead to the formation of an abscess, often accompanied by great abdominal distension. In favourable cases an incision outside the limits of the peritoneal cavity may be possible and prove successful.

Stomach.—Intervention is rarely called for unless a subphrenic abscess develops. Wounds of the stomach may be closed spontaneously by adhesion. In such cases serious secondary hæmorrhage may occur at the end of a week or later ; hence care in feeding is essential.

Small Intestine.—Few cases of perforation of the small intestine survive, and still fewer arrive at the Base in a condition in which operation should be considered. It may happen that a loop of wounded small intestine has prolapsed and a fæcal fistula has been established ; here a secondary resection has been followed by cure.

Colon.—A considerable number of patients with wounds of the colon arrive at the base hospitals often in good condition. Either a fæcal fistula has been established, or the colon has become adherent to the abdominal parietes and some local inflammatory signs will be detectable. In the latter case an expectant attitude is to be maintained ; in a few cases spontaneous healing may result, in others a secondary local abscess may develop and need incision. Frequently a fæcal fistula will open when the first action of the bowels takes place.

Fæcal fistula.

The treatment of the fæcal fistula differs, according to the amount of intestinal contents which escapes and with the nature of the wound and its position. If the fistula is small, and especially if the anterior aspect of the bowel furnishes the discharge, the expectant attitude should be maintained, and the fistula may heal.

Treatment of fæcal fistula.

If the opening is large and particularly if the wound in the abdominal parietes is deep, irregular, or complicated by the co-existence of a fracture of a rib or the pelvis, a proximal temporary colostomy should be made, and the passage of the fæces through the wound arrested; otherwise the patient will die from local extension of the infection and general sapræmia or septicæmia. Colostomy.

Unfortunately this plan is not practicable in the case of the ascending colon or cæcum, the parts most commonly the seat of isolated injury.

In considering the question of an early temporary colostomy care must always be taken to exclude the presence of coexistent injury to the small intestine, which not rarely exists when the path taken by the bullet is oblique.

Rectum.—Large wounds of the rectum, especially when complicated by fracture of the pelvis, should be treated by a temporary inguinal or transverse colostomy. Small wounds of the lower part of the rectum may be successfully treated by free division of the sphincter ani, to produce temporary incontinence and hence make the path by the anus the most easy for the passage of flatus and fæces. Treatment of wounds of the rectum.

Wounds of the rectum complicated by wound of the bladder constitute a difficult problem; they occasionally heal spontaneously. If operation is considered advisable, the special measure should be a colostomy, in the hope that the wound in the bladder may heal spontaneously. The bladder and colon must not both be opened at the same time. Wounds of the rectum and bladder.

Liver.—Many patients with rifle bullet wounds traversing the liver arrive at the base without any troublesome symptoms, or physical signs indicative of the injury.

This is not so with those caused by fragments of shell or shrapnel case. In such, jaundice and signs of effusion of bile, or a mixture of bile and blood into the peritoneal or pleural cavities are not uncommon. The effusion is infected, and death from septic absorption or secondary hæmorrhage is common. Again, the presence of a septic foreign body may give rise to an hepatic or subphrenic abscess. Operative interference is only indicated in the fortunate cases in which a localized hepatic, or intraperitoneal abscess forms ; in these instances, if a foreign body is present, it may be discovered and removed when the abscess is opened.

Subphrenic abscess.

The presence of a biliary fistula is in itself of little importance ; such fistulæ, even when the bile traverses the pleura, usually heal spontaneously.

Biliary fistula.

Kidneys.—Wounds of the kidney may need surgical interference for the relief of urinary extravasation or hæmorrhage. Pure urinary extravasation rarely occurs, but in large wounds of the loin, and especially if the pelvis or the kidney is wounded, an abundant flow of urine may result. If the egress is free, the urinary fistula is commonly of short duration ; the wound heals as after an operation on the kidney. If the egress of the urine is checked by narrowness or obliquity of the wound, the urine may follow the course of the ureter to the iliac fossa and pelvis, or become extravasated into the tissues of the back. In such cases free incision may be required, and rarely any interference with the kidney itself.

Extravasation of urine.

Renal hæmorrhage is a matter of greater importance. It may take the form of hæmaturia, or retroperitoneal hæmorrhage, but the two are often combined. Gross primary hæmaturia is not a constant sign of renal injury ; it is not infrequently absent. If present it may persist for a few days and then cease spontaneously. If profuse and persistent, the kidney must be explored and may need to be removed.

Renal hæmorrhage.

Secondary hæmaturia, coming on from the fifth to the tenth day, is a more serious condition; commonly it results from septic infection and tends to persist. If the loss of blood is great and continued, the kidney will probably have to be sacrificed.

Peri-renal retroperitoneal hæmorrhage may also be primary or secondary. The blood extravasation tends to spread in the line of the ureter, and a hard mass, dull to percussion, often accompanied by superficial ecchymsois and œdema, occupies the loin and iliac fossa. Such blood effusions should not be interfered with unless they are increasing and causing dangerous anæmia, or if they become infected, threaten suppuration, or actually suppurate. In either case incision is necessary. If hæmorrhage is persisting the kidney must be explored and dealt with; if suppuration is the indication simple incision and drainage of the collection may suffice. The question of treatment of the kidney itself is one of some difficulty; the organ may be in fragments, widely fissured, cut in twain, or merely grooved or perforated. In the latter cases, if the operation is performed at an early stage and in the absence of infection, the advisability of suture of the wound or partial removal of the organ may be considered.

If the kidney is hopelessly damaged it must be removed. If the hæmorrhage has been secondary in character the same course must be pursued, even if the wound be small, since it is obvious that in a patient already anæmic no further risk of recurrence can be taken. The rigid nature of the fatty capsule, infiltrated with blood and urine, and its firm adherence to the kidney may render the operation, especially the delivery of the organ and ligature of the pedicle, a procedure of considerable difficulty.

The lumbar route is obviously the best and safest for the operation.

Bladder.—Few cases of intraperitoneal injury to the bladder reach the base hospitals, unless they have been operated upon. Extraperitoneal injuries are common, some giving rise neither to leakage nor extravasation, others leaking freely or accompanied by extraperitoneal hypogastric extravasation. The urinary fistulæ are most common in the hypogastrium, the buttock, the side of the pelvis, or the thigh. While the urine remains uninfected the patients suffer little, and those that are left to be operated upon at the base do better than those in whom the presence of urgent conditions has necessitated an operation prior to their transference. In the latter case a tendency to lateral extravasation from the suprapubic wound is not infrequently observed.

Extraperitoneal wounds of the bladder.

In instances where the extravasation of urine is localized and of some standing, a simple hypogastric incision suffices to cure the condition, as the opening into the bladder has already contracted or even closed. When this is not the case, the best course is to perform a suprapubic cystotomy, the original wound into the bladder being utilized, if possible, for the tube.

Treatment of extravasation of urine.

Catheters should not be tied in, as cystitis follows and probably infection of the open wound track, with its attendant dangers.

The operation of cystotomy has been one of those most uniformly satisfactory in results of the whole campaign. Coexistent injury of the bladder and rectum has already been dealt with under the heading of the latter organ (*see* page 99).

INJURIES TO THE MEMBRANA TYM-PANI DUE TO SHELL EXPLOSIONS.

In these injuries the deep meatus and the broken tympanic membrane must be left absolutely at rest. A light application of 2 per cent iodine solution in spirit should be made to the cartilaginous portion of the external auditory meatus, care being taken that none of the fluid reaches the deeper part of the canal. The outer part of the meatus should then be plugged lightly with cotton wool.

Syringing or the introduction of drops of lotions, especially hydrogen peroxide, are all dangerous. Such applications, beyond being painful, are very apt to give rise to acute inflammation of the middle ear, or actual suppuration.

INJURIES TO THE EYES.

Immediate Treatment.—The lids and parts around the eye should be cleansed, and the conjunctival sac washed out with—if possible—sterilised boric acid lotion or saline solution to remove discharge or any loose foreign matter, and some sterilised 1 per cent. atropin ointment inserted between the lids. If no such ointment be at hand, ophthalmic tablets can be used, though these cause more irritation, are more difficult to manipulate, and are by no means always sterile. The eye is covered with a sterilised pad and bandaged, till a complete examination can be made (*see below*).

Castor oil should not be used if there is a penetrating wound of the eye.

General considerations.
Though the bulk of ophthalmic injuries met with in warfare are so severe that the damaged eye has to be removed to prevent the risk of sympathetic ophthalmia in its fellow, yet there are certain cases in which the eye can be saved by prompt and careful treatment. Not all the eyes which are blind need be removed, whereas many eyes which have vision may lead, if incorrectly treated, to complete blindness of both. When one eye only is injured our main object must be to keep the other sound, and to run no risk of sympathetic ophthalmia. The two questions that have constantly to be decided are :—

1. Will the injured eye be a useful organ of vision, and
2. Will it be a menace to its fellow.

Sympathetic ophthalmia never follows a non-penetrating injury. All merely bruised eyes can therefore be left with safety. Penetrating wounds are the menace, and difficulty arises where there is no obvious perforation, in excluding the possibility of a small foreign body having been driven into the eye ; hence the importance of the following careful examination.

Examination of injured eyes.—1. Look for wounds in parts around, *e.g.*, lids, temple, brow or cheek, indicating entrance of a foreign body which may have passed into the globe.

2. **Proptosis** may be due to a foreign body in the orbit, hæmorrhage or cellulitis or panophthalmitis.

3. **Cornea**, search for foreign bodies or wounds with or without prolapse or entanglement of iris or lens capsule.

4. **Sclera.**—Look for foreign bodies, wounds or rupture with or without prolapse of ciliary body or choroid.

5. **Anterior chamber.**—Hyphæma, hypopyon or foreign body.

6. **Iris.**—Pupil circular or irregular ; reaction to light ; rupture of sphincter ; tearing away from periphery (iridodialysis), or a hole due to a foreign body having penetrated. Discoloration or muddiness indicating iritis or panophthalmitis.

7. **Tension.**—A very soft eye following immediately after injury usually points to a wound or rupture ; but this is not diagnostic, for an eye which is merely badly bruised may have a much reduced tension.

8. **Vision**, should be tested and recorded. If very poor the field of vision should be taken roughly with the hand, and the projection of light tried.

Dilate the pupil when necessary and examine ;

9. **The red reflex**, and see if it can be obtained in all or only some directions.

10. **Lens.**—For dislocation, cataract, or track of a foreign body.

11. **Vitreous.**—For hæmorrhage or foreign body ; a yellow reflex indicates panophthalmitis.

12. **Fundus.**—For signs of concussion (hæmorrhage in the retina, or gross white patches, etc.); rupture of choroid, detachment of retina, or foreign body.

13. **An X-ray photograph** should be taken.

Conclusions to be drawn from examination.

Having finished the examination it must be decided (*a*) what is a useful eye, and (*b*) what eye is a menace.

(*a*) If there is perception of light and good projection there is a possibility of a serviceable eye. Concussion of the retina and hæmorrhage into the vitreous lower the acuity greatly, but these effects may clear up and a surprising amount of vision return.

(*b*) Dangerous eyes are those in which there is a rupture or penetrating wound of the globe, and especially when complicated with a prolapse of iris, ciliary body, choroid or lens capsule. Suppurating eyes (panophthalmitis) very rarely cause sympathetic ophthalmia, whereas chronic inflammation of the iris or ciliary body (plastic iridocyclitis) as a result of penetrating injury, and particularly if associated with Keratitis Punctata, is the condition par excellence which is the precursor of sympathetic inflammation and blindness.

Sympathetic ophthalmia.

Sympathetic ophthalmia does not occur earlier than ten days after injury, and rarely before three weeks, so that we may take ten to fourteen days to be the conventional period of safety in which to decide the fate of an eye. It is, however, a golden rule to decide as soon as possible in order to avoid risk, and to remove an eye as soon as it is condemned.

Complications of injuries.

Ruptured eyes.—(1). When only one eye is ruptured and blind, it should be removed without delay, certainly within the first ten days after injury; however badly disorganized, the remains should not be left (*see* excision).

(2) When both eyes are ruptured and blind, on the other hand, no operation should be undertaken im-

mediately, unless they are causing very great pain, or for some reason life is endangered by keeping the remains; neither of which conditions are likely to occur. It serves no useful purpose to inflict the depression, which would follow the knowledge that both organs of sight have been taken away immediately after the shock of injury. Such patients may be told that both eyes have been badly bruised, and they will gradually come to the knowledge that the rest of their life is to be spent in darkness. Exception may be made in the case of those transverse wounds of the head where one eye is whole, though blind from concussion or division of the optic nerve, and the other blind from rupture or wound. The latter should be removed to prevent sympathetic inflammation in its fellow.

Penetrating wounds with prolapse of iris, ciliary body, or choroid.—If the eye is blind, it should be excised, but if there is useful vision, an attempt should be made to remove the prolapse. *These latter cases should only be operated upon by those who have special ophthalmic knowledge,* and who have the necessary instruments for the purpose. Properly dealt with they form one of the few opportunities for conservative ophthalmic surgery in warfare, while an incomplete interference will almost certainly prevent a satisfactory secondary operation being performed. They should, as a rule, therefore, be sent immediately to the base, and the ophthalmic surgeon notified without delay. The sooner the operation is undertaken the more likely will the uveal tissue be cleanly removed from the lips of the wound; the longer the interval the tougher will be the adhesions. It must be always borne in mind that a penetrating wound of the globe following an explosion is practically a proof that a foreign body has entered or passed through the eye; a

I

skiagram should, therefore, be taken in every case. (For the treatment of foreign body in the eye, see below.)

Prolapse of iris.—In operating on a prolapse our endeavour must be to pull out the iris so freely, that after cutting, the pillars of the iris retract away from the wound. Our aim is to leave not only no prolapse or entanglement, but not even an adhesion. An adhesion is a source of irritation and delays quiescence, while an entanglement is a positive danger, and will demand further operation.

A gaping wound of the cornea cannot be sutured, but may be covered with a flap of conjunctiva.

Prolapse of the ciliary body or choroid.—If clean, this should be replaced and the sclera brought together with sutures ; if it is ragged or obviously infected, it should be drawn out and excised before suturing. (N.B.—In suturing the sclera, a double-needled thread should be used, and the needles passed from within outwards through the superficial part of the sclera, taking great care not to include any uveal tissue, the lips of the wound being firmly held in toothed forceps to prevent escape of vitreous while passing the needle.)

Penetrating wounds without prolapse of uveal tissue.—If the eye is blind it should be excised. If there is a chance of saving useful vision the sclera should be sutured ; gaping wounds of the margin of the cornea may be covered with a flap of conjunctiva as described above.

Foreign bodies in the cornea.—When deeply embedded these are often curiously troublesome to remove. A Beer's knife is the most useful instrument to employ, a needle is not stiff enough ; a bright light should be well focussed on the cornea, and it is a great help to work under a magnifying glass. When the foreign bodies are very numerous, and are not causing irritation, they should be left alone and the cornea treated as if it had been tattooed. If they are causing irritation each one must be picked out.

Foreign bodies in the eye or orbit.—If there is any suspicion that a foreign body is in the eye or orbit a skiagram should be taken. If its presence is proved, it should be localized by Mackenzie Davidson's method to ascertain whether it be in or outside the eye.

Foreign bodies in the orbit set up more or less severe cellulitis, with proptosis and limitation of ocular movement. With the smaller fragments the cellulitis soon subsides under fomentations, and the fragments can be left; when severe it must be treated by incision, drainage and removal of the fragments.

Foreign bodies in the eye.—This group is the most unsatisfactory with which one has to deal, for many of the foreign bodies are non-magnetic. Present experience shows that more harm is done by blindly searching than in leaving them alone. (How far the telephone probe and forceps or the large magnet will help us remains to be seen.) A foreign body in the eye which is not complicated with prolapse of uvea or of the lens capsule, or with chronic iridocyclitis, does not lead to sympathetic ophthalmia; on the other hand the eye is very likely to degenerate. If the eye is blind, it should be removed, but while the eye remains quiet and has useful vision it should be left; if, however, it remains irritable or becomes blind it should be removed forthwith.

The complication of prolapse of uveal tissue is a serious one, but if as stated above this can be cleanly removed and the wound sutured or covered with conjunctiva, it may be treated on the lines indicated, but the risk being

I 2

greater, the period of waiting for the eye to quiet down must be correspondingly shortened.

It is essential that all cases of penetrating injury with or without foreign body, in which the eye has been left and is on its probation, should be kept under careful supervision of an ophthalmic surgeon. In evacuating to England, these cases should therefore be labelled specially to be sent to an ophthalmic hospital or the ophthalmic department of a general hospital.

Method of excision of the eye in the presence of orbital cellulitis or panophthalmitis.—If the eye is excised in the ordinary way with division of the optic nerve in the presence of orbital cellulitis, or where there is panophthalmitis, a definite risk is run of causing septic meningitis and death.

The following modification will be found a simple procedure and one free from risk :—

1. The contents of the globe are thoroughly eviscerated, all traces of retina and choroid being scraped away to avoid any chance of sympathetic ophthalmia.

2. The muscles are divided.

3. The sclerotic is pulled forward and divided far back, leaving only a frill round the intact optic nerve. The actual procedure may be varied according to the following circumstances :—

Method of excision.

(a) When the opening in the globe is small or has firmly healed and the contents are not septic, the conjunctiva and muscles are divided first, as this is of course much more simply done while there is some tension in the globe. The cornea is then cut away and the contents of the eye carefully scraped out, either with a large sharp spoon or with a scoop made for the purpose, and the process completed by scrubbing out the sclera with a swab held in a pair of forceps. The sclerotic is drawn well forward by two or three pairs of pressure forceps and cut far back, leaving a frill round the nerve as described above.

(*b*) If there is panophthalmitis, the cornea is first removed by transfixing and cutting upwards and removing the lower half with scissors. The contents are completely scraped out as described above, and the shell of sclerotic and conjunctiva thoroughly washed. The sclerotic is now packed firmly with a strip of gauze to facilitate the division of the muscles, which is next performed. The gauze is then removed, the sclera drawn well forward and divided as before.

The same method applies in the case of an open wound or rent of the eye.

(*c*) Where the globe is split open in many directions, as is often the case when a bullet has passed through it, packing is impossible. In this case, after scooping and wiping out the contents of the eye, the separate portions of the sclera can be picked up and made taut with pressure forceps and the muscles dissected off. After drawing the bunch of forceps forward the sclerotic is now cut through as described above.

The three points to keep in mind are :—

1. To remove all traces of retina or choroid.
2. To take away the bulk of the sclerotic, but,
3. To leave a frill of sclerotic round the intact optic nerve.

In this way all risk of infection of the nerve sheath and the meninges as the result of the operation is avoided ; there is very little bleeding, the shock due to cutting the optic nerve does not occur, drainage for the cellulitis is afforded, and the healing process is not prolonged by leaving the bulk of the sclerotic as in ordinary evisceration.

TRENCH FOOT. FROST BITE.

Cases described under these headings were very numerous during the Winter of 1914–1915, and were observed well into the following spring. They were practically limited to men standing in water in the trenches, other troops were not affected to any material extent.

The frequency and the severity of the cases were alike in direct proportion to the length of time men had to stay in trenches ; and when, for military reasons, the stay was necessarily prolonged for several days and nights consecutively at a temperature below 40 F., men and officers alike were often incapacitated for several months.

Although the predisposing cause appears to have been prolonged exposure to a low temperature, not necessarily near freezing point, and wet, the most aggravated cases occurred in men who remained on duty in the trenches without removing boots or puttees for several days at a time. Constriction of the circulation in the lower limbs is therefore to be regarded as the most important exciting cause, and this is accentuated by wearing tight boots and puttees, prolonged strain and standing, and possibly nerve strain. Many of the worst cases were met with in men who had to lie out for long periods after being wounded, often without food.

In the slighter cases the feet presented no obvious changes, but anæsthesia of the functional type was present, or the feet were œdematous, and definite organic sensory changes could be detected.

In more severe cases, marked cyanosis, gross œdema, bleb formation, and serious organic sensory changes were present. In these a prolonged period of rest and

Variations in degree.

treatment was required before the men were fit to return to duty.

In the worst cases, dry gangrene of the frost bite type developed, leading to the death of considerable areas of skin, the loss of one or more toes, or massive gangrene of the feet, even extending to the lower third of the leg.

Similar conditions were more rarely observed in the hands. Definite patches of gangrene over prominent bony points as the front of the knees, or over areas exposed to pressure as the outer aspect of the thigh, in men who had lain out on the field for long periods, were also occasionally seen.

The feet are likely to be affected under the following circumstances :—

1. When the boots and puttees are too tight.

2. When the general circulation throughout the body is less active than normal.

3. When socks, boots and puttees are wet.

The following precautions have been recommended as prophylactic measures :—

1. Boots should not fit tightly, but should be at least a size too large. When boots are large enough it is well to wear two pairs of socks ; but this is dangerous if the boots are small, as it leads to further pressure on the feet. Puttees should never be applied tightly. *Prophylactic measures.*

2. The general circulation can be kept up by keeping the body warm and dry. A mackintosh sheet worn over the greatcoat is of assistance where no waterproof is available.

3. A dry pair of socks should be carried in the pockets when available.

4. Boots and puttees should be taken off at least once in 24 hours, the feet rubbed and dried and a dry pair of socks put on.

5. Boots should be well greased or dubbined.

Officers should see that dry standing is provided in the trenches whenever possible, by means of drainage, raising of the foot level by fascines of brushwood or straw with boards on top, or by the use of pumps where these are available.

Curative treatment. The curative methods consist in rest and elevation of the feet. In the early stages the feet should be bandaged with a covering of wool. Later, in the hyperæsthetic stage the feet should be uncovered.

The formation of bullæ is often accompanied by a very sharp rise of temperature. The bullæ should be punctured as the fluid is commonly infected with anaerobes or other organisms.

Counter-irritant treatment has met with little success, but in the slighter cases massage and Faradism have been useful. Pain may be relieved by the administration of aspirin. Convalescence in the more severe cases is often very protracted.

Massive gangrene is usually of the dry type, in which event amputation should be deferred until the patients reach England. Occasionally it may assume the moist type with grave signs of constitutional infection; prompt amputation is then indicated.

GAS-POISONING.

Nature of the gas.— Injurious gases are of two classes, "drift gas" and "shell gas." The former is discharged from cylinders and other apparatus placed in the enemy trenches. Chlorine is certainly a chief constituent of the drift gas, though other substances may be present, but the evidence on this question is still indirect. The gas produces effects similar to those caused by chlorine, and chlorides have been found as a deposit on the buttons of "gassed" men. But the gas itself has not yet been collected and analysed. There is no reason to believe that different gases have been used in different attacks. Two different gases. Drift gas.

The asphyxiating shells contain other substances. Some are irritant like chlorine, but other effects are produced, such as stupor, and temporary blindness by excessive irritation of the eyes. A peculiar vasodilator substance has also been observed. Shell gas.

Pathological changes.—These have been ascertained by autopsies made on a large number of fatal cases, which were presumably all caused by drift gas. The following description applies only to the results of that gas. Pathological changes.

Although the great majority of the cases are mild, the condition produced may sometimes be of great severity. There are three successive stages of injury produced by the poison, at any one of which death is possible.

1. The first is apparently that of direct poisoning. Death during it occurs in the first few hours. The face of the sufferer is greenish-yellow and pallid. No post- Three successive stages.

mortem examinations have been made on cases of death during this earliest stage.

2. The second is that of œdema of the lungs, with general asphyxia. Livid cyanosis with great dyspnœa is the outstanding clinical feature. Death in this stage may occur at any time from the first to the fourth or fifth day.

3. During the third, secondary infections of the bronchial passages and lungs may develop, causing purulent bronchitis, broncho-pneumonia, pleurisy, or even empyema and gangrene of the lung. These may be fatal in the second or third week.

Most men who have survived to the third week have recovered, at any rate, from the acute illness.

Effects on the respiratory organs.

The Lungs.— Acute emphysema is one of the first changes. The lungs may actually bulge out of the chest when the sternum is removed. The vesicles burst and air escapes into the interstitial tissues, so that bubbles of air are found in the mediastinum, and in some cases even the neck and upper part of the chest may be distended with subcutaneous emphysema.

An intense and universal œdema of the lungs develops side by side with the emphysema as the result of the irritant action of the gas on the bronchi and alveolar epithelium. A yellow serous fluid fills the air passages in such quantities that it may drip from the mouth of the living patient when the stretcher is tilted head downwards. The combined result of this œdema, together with scattered areas of collapse and of disruptive emphysema, is such that the lungs can with difficulty transmit the circulating blood, and that they entirely fail to carry out the necessary gaseous exchanges with the air. Petechial, or larger subpleural, hæmorrhages are seen scattered over the surface of the lungs, and they are probably caused by the general asphyxiation. Deeper areas of ordinary infarction also occur.

In addition to the hæmorrhages there are often separate blebs caused by subpleural collections of inflammatory fluid.

The trachea and base of the tongue are at first of a deep purple red colour from congestive irritation There is no obstructive œdema of the laryngeal aperture.

In the third stage the serous exudate is found to be in part re-absorbed, especially at the periphery of the lungs. Instead of frothy serum the bronchi and trachea now contain a purulent secretion, scattered areas of broncho-pneumonia or a general imperfect consolidation are seen, and a rough pleurisy coats the surface.

Other organs.—The changes in these are of less clinical importance. The heart is engorged and may show epicardial hæmorrhages. All the great veins are over distended with black clotted blood. The liver and spleen merely show venous engorgement. The kidneys are gorged with blood, but there is at the same time a toxic nephritis which may be very apparent to the naked eye in those who die late in the second week. Under the microscope the tubules are found to be more swollen and affected than are the glomeruli.

The stomach, especially at the cardiac end, is dotted with petechial hæmorrhages, and these may enlarge to a superficial erosion of such an extent that in some cases the stomach after death has been found to be full of effused blood.

No changes other than those of asphyxia have been observed in the brain.

To summarise, the main effect is that of a mechanical asphyxia caused by irritative œdema and disruptive emphysema of the pulmonary air cells. The gas does not

118

interfere with the respiratory properties of the hæmo-globin or blood plasma, and no greater acidosis has been found in the blood than that which would correspond to the loss of oxygen and excess of carbon dioxide due to the high degree of asphyxia present.

The changes in the kidneys, however, prove that a poison has been absorbed into the circulating blood ; and probably the lesions in the stomach are caused in the same way.

Clinical features.—The poisonous results of the " drift " gas may be grouped under three headings.

    1. Those due to irritation of the respiratory tract.

    2. Those due to gastric irritation.

    3. General toxic effects.

Symptoms. Exposure to the gas causes immediate choking, gasping, and coughing. The throat burns and the eyes smart, while there is often free lachrymation. Pain is felt behind the sternum, and this may become very severe as it extends outwards into each side of the chest.

Retching soon follows, and a greenish-yellow fluid is brought up. There is rarely any bleeding from the nose. The feeling of dyspnœa is soon overborne by the general toxic effects. The man's head aches ; his legs feel weak, and instead of sitting up in urgent efforts to breathe, he yields to an overpowering sense of fatigue and lies prone upon the earth. This position is peculiarly dangerous, since the heavy gas lies in greatest concentration on the folds and recesses of the ground. In many cases there is not only stupefaction but an actual loss of consciousness, that may persist for hours.

Occasionally a deeper stupor has been observed for two or three days in men who showed relatively few respira-tory symptoms. This may have been. a phenomenon peculiar to the individual, and there is no reason to believe that a gas with purely narcotizing effects has been employed on any occasion by the enemy, unless the stupor was caused by special gases emitted from bursting shells.

Little is known about the worst cases which succumb on the field. In addition to dyspnœa they are characterized by a greenish yellow colour of the face which underlies the distended venules, a state of asphyxia pallida that indicates final failure of the heart and invariably heralds death. *Death on the field.*

From the clearing stations onwards the sufferers can be divided into two main groups, (*a*) those with asphyxial lividity, and (*b*) those with only a few physical signs in the lungs. Both have marked dyspnœa, and this respiratory hurry, though the patient is often hardly aware of it, together with fine râles at the bases of the lungs, provides the chief clinical proof that the soldier has been "gassed." *Physical signs and symptoms.*

(*a*) Cyanosis is seen in the face, ears, and finger nails. The colour is reddish blue, changing to a leaden hue when death is imminent. On the lips there are dry sordes, but never herpetic blisters. The tongue is caked with a leathery dry fur, and the roof of the palate is often glazed and dry.

The pulse is regular, full, and rarely more than 100. The respiration is shallow and extraordinarily rapid, up to 60 or even 80 a minute. Often the chest is held in a position of extreme distension, and the forced respiratory movements appear only in the diaphragm and the accessory muscles at the upper inlet. The percussion note is everywhere resonant, even, on account of the scattered emphysema, over the bases which autopsy proves to be almost solid with œdema. The breath sounds may be harsh, but are never tubular. Very characteristic is the presence of innumerable fine crepitant râles, especially at the back and sides. Rhonchi are occasionally heard.

There is frequent and painful cough, with the expectoration of a viscid, primrose-yellow sputum, that is often streaked with blood from the trachea, or reddish-brown from infarcted areas within. Pain is complained of in the epigastrium as well as in the chest. The former may have been caused by the muscular strain of coughing, but it is sometimes of gastric origin and aggravated by food. Headache is invariably present, and the patient generally lies more or less prostrate in bed, though fully conscious.

In most cases lividity disappears within two or three days, but any muscular effort will at once restore a cyanotic tint to the face. The unconscious hurry of the respiration still persists, and its cause lies partly in a protracted acidosis of the blood, partly in the fact that the deeper masses of the lung are still œdematous and useless for aeration. A deep breath will reveal fine râles at the bases for many days.

The temperature is raised to 100° or 101° F. at first, but it soon falls except where secondary infections are developing. Then the expectoration becomes purulent and even nummular : the physical signs in the lungs persist, and are aggravated in accordance with the nature of the subsequent pathological changes.

Despite the post-mortem evidence of renal changes, there is rarely albuminuria or any clinical evidence of damage to the kidneys. There is no peripheral neuritis, and the nervous system shows no symptoms other than the headache and general lassitude.

A few cases have suffered from circulatory obstruction in the feet and hands. In these the extremities became painful, livid, and cold ; but the condition slowly cleared up, and actual gangrene did not result.

(b) Headache, pain in the chest, and hurried respiration are the chief features. On auscultation fine râles are heard at the base and side of the lungs, and at a later time rhonchi over the front of the chest.

The condition rapidly clears up, but the patient suffers *Prognosis.* from headache, weakness in the legs, vomiting and sometimes epistaxis if he is compelled to leave bed too early A dry pleurisy may develop in these cases, but the more serious and deeper infections are rarely to be feared.

The total mortality before the use of efficient respirators *Mortality.* was about 6 per cent in the patients who arrived at the clearing stations, but the number of those who died in the trenches is unknown. Of those which reached the base hospitals only 1 or 2 per cent succumbed.

Treatment.—Men must be thoroughly trained in the *Prophy-* use of efficient helmets, and cautioned that these are not *lactic* to be removed until they are out of the danger zone. *precautions.* Even the simple type of respirator first used was found to prevent the red injection of the trachea, and thanks to it the late secondary infections, if they occurred, were not fatal.

In the first twenty-four hours the aim of treatment *Treatment.* must be to check bronchial spasm and lessen the œdematous flooding of the lungs. Atropine should be given in doses of 1/100 grain 4 hourly. Ammonium carbonate in doses of 10 grains every six hours is also useful. Many patients vomit spontaneously or provoke vomiting in themselves. This relieves the stomach, and it may help to empty the lungs temporarily. Emetics may be tried for the same purpose. Chloroform, ether, and alcohol only allay the bronchial irritation and spasm to a slight degree, and they are otherwise dangerous. Oxygen inhalation is useful.

From the second day onwards the œdema of the lungs is established and the bronchial spasm has ceased. Extreme cyanosis with a full pulse requires venesection to about 15 ounces. Oxygen gives some relief, though it does not reduce the lividity. It should be supplied through a tube within the patient's mouth.

The majority of "gassed" men feel easier when they are placed in a tent with a steam kettle containing Tinct. Benzoin Co. Others, however, dislike this, and prefer the free air near a window or outside the building. Potassium iodide in small doses may be given later, and stimulating expectorants if the sputum becomes purulent. The food should be light or fluid, in view of the lesions that occur in the stomach.

Prognosis.

Except where secondary infections occur, the men who have escaped death in the first few days recover quickly and, so far as is known, completely. Those in whom marked lividity was present should be sent to England for a long rest. Others are fit for duty in a shorter time.

Date for return to duty.

All cases should remain in hospital until the fine râles have vanished from the axillæ and bases of the lungs. Lassitude and fatigue tend to persist for some time, so that those who have been "gassed" cannot resume heavy work at once.

INDEX.

A.

K

ND - #0508 - 270225 - C0 - 132/107/13 - PB - 9781908487919 - Matt Lamination